RICHARD MOREHEAD'S

TEXAS

Feb. 2, 1982

To ████████ —
With hope you will
enjoy these true tales of Texas
Sincerely
Richard M. Morehead

RICHARD MOREHEAD'S
TEXAS

Armadillos, Lawmakers
Wild Turkeys, Writers,

And Other Texas Miscellanea

Graphics By
James Loehlin

EAKIN PRESS   BURNET, TEXAS

Published in the United States of America
By Eakin Publications, Inc., P.O. Drawer AG,
Burnet, Texas 78611

ISBN 0-89015-306-X

To My Wife
Judith
My most constant reader and honest critic.

TABLE OF CONTENTS

I. Armadillos and Assorted Texas Critters

II. All You Want To Know About Overalls and More

III. Eggnog And Chitterlings

IV. Weather, Water And Oil — Texas Style

PREFACE

Although Richard Morehead is best known as a writer for *The Dallas Morning News* on politics, government, energy, civil rights, and education, there is another side to the author and to the many subjects he has treated.

His columns in recent years have dealt increasingly with interesting people, rural and outdoor Texas, and the memorable details of everyday life.

Besides *The Dallas Morning News,* Morehead's work has appeared over the years in many national and state magazines, *The National Observer,* and other newspapers. With his wife, Judith, the author has written *The Texas Wild Game Cookbook,* and he has written for *The Texas Almanac* and other books on state government.

Most of Morehead's comments on politics and politicians he has known are reserved for a future book. Herein are recorded some observations: J. Frank Dobie's last interview, J. Evetts Haley, Wick Fowler, DeWitt C. Reddick, the great journalism teacher, and other special people.

They are included with the author's running war with woodpeckers, his romance with the wild turkey, his father's famous Four Roses eggnog recipe, and Sam Wood's corn bread cooking.

Most of Morehead's career has been spent writing about serious, even dreary, affairs. This one reflects the other side of a newsman's job, and of the writer's nature.

I

Armadillos and Assorted Texas Critters

THE TEXAS STATE MAMMAL

Because Texas senators disagreed, the 9-banded armadillo lost its chance in 1981 to become the official "state mammal."

The resolution by Rep. Don Henderson of Houston breezed through the House of Representatives, but senators balked when an anti-armadillo lobby attempted to substitute the opossum, longhorn cow, unicorn, or buffalo as the official Texas animal.

Whether you agree that Texas need the armadillo as an official symbol of Texas — along with the bluebonnet, the mockingbird, pecan tree and chili — the students of Oak Creek Elementary School in Houston deserve an A-plus for effort.

They researched the armadillo, had a resolution introduced two years ago which failed in the legislature's session-end rush, and this time came back with a lobby that included students from other Texas public schools.

The armadillo is described in the resolution, which the Oak Creek scholars wrote, as a "hardy, pioneering creature that chose to begin migrating here about the time Texas became a state . . . "

While we have never regarded the armadillo as all that heroic a figure, we admire the sponsors' ingenuity and would do nothing to stand in the way of honoring this ugly, mostly harmless animal.

The armadillo's following is mostly among the urban cowboy crowd, that has become so enthusiastic about its mascot the legislature had to pass a law two years ago outlawing the sale or possession for sale of a live armadillo (or skunk).

Rep. Bill Hollowell of Grand Saline and Sen. Roy Blake of Nacogdoches sponsored the armadillo-skunk protection act, making violation a misdemeanor subjecting offenders to six months in jail and $1,500 fine.

Local law officers probably look the other way when armadillo races are run, theorizing the strange little nearsighted animals aren't really ''possessed for sale'' by a human just because it is brought to town for the races.

The 9-banded armadillo's biological name is *dasypus novemcinctus Mexicanus,* meaning it originated in Mexico.

Armadillos have been around South and Central Texas all my life. The Armadillo World Headquarters was established in Austin a few years ago, a beer and rock music center, but was torn down before I could muster courage to attend any performances.

Armadillos dig holes everywhere, a reason they prefer cultivated gardens and flower beds to rocky soil. They eat grubs, worms, small lizards, and some plants.

While some professed armadillo lovers recoil at the thought, they are good to eat. The meat is light and tender, like turtle, pheasant, or young chicken. Getting one ready for the table is a chore, for the tough underside is difficult to separate from the shell.

There is a story abroad that armadillos carry leprosy, which would be a good reason to avoid them. However, Dr. Orville Wyss, an eminent microbiologist at The University of Texas and sometimes armadillo observer, says there's no proof a human can catch leprosy from eating an armadillo or associating with one.

There's no reason to fear an armadillo unless you try to pick one up in a manner where the claws can scratch you.

Horsemen dislike armadillo areas because a horse can be injured stepping into an armadillo hole.

Armadillos do not need to swim. They can walk under a creek or pond without drowning, we are told.

Horace Gore, a Texas Parks and Wildlife specialist, defends the armadillo against the charge it eats eggs of quail, wild turkeys, and other birds. Gore reports the animal will eat only a broken egg and will never break one on purpose.

Armadillos are used for medical and genetic research, because each litter contains four usually identical offspring.

In nature, armadillos seem to be abundant or scarce without any easy explanation. Once I asked my friend Claud Gilmer of Rocksprings why there were so many armadillos that season.

''It was just a good year for armadillos,'' he explained.

DECLARING WAR ON WOODPECKERS

A private war with woodpeckers highlighted one year-end vacation.

For several years, these pesky peckers had been drilling holes in our cabin in the Lampasas Hill Country. We thought that some year, surely, they would seek a healthier residence than an ancient attic.

Instead, the woodpeckers seem to be telling their friends about the place. ''They think your cabin is a big hollow log,'' chortled a bystander.

Two woodpeckers met their maker during the latest match, but others are still sounding a rat-a-tat-tat on the ancient lumber. Both recent victims came down the chimney of our little 2-hole wood heating stove. One made the fatal journey while the coals were still burning. It lay barbecued in the ashes when we arrived.

But inside was another still alive, a Yellow-Shafted Flicker, according to a bird expert. The moment we opened the stove door, Ms. Flicker flicked into the kitchen and made several laps among the pots and pans before being felled with a cardboard swatter. The name of the successful marksman will remain anonymous for fear the yellow-shafted flicker is on somebody's protected list.

It took a couple of hours to clean up the place, for ashes had settled all over our 3-room abode. This was only the latest of depredations by the durable bird, which had managed to peck numerous holes in the 1-inch boards siding the cabin. It must be added that the lumber is so old and hard that a carpenter has difficulty driving a nail into it, so woodpeckers must use diamond drills.

The woodpeckers get an ''A'' for effort. On a previous occasion three came down our chimney together and expired within the stove during our absence. Another time, a large woodpecker managed to beat open the stove door and spend a few messy days within the house before dropping dead in the living room. Its telltale purple stains remain on the curtains.

This winter, after hammering two holes for the bird family to move into the attic, our woodpecker adversaries airlifted large chunks of the insulation from the attic into the yard. Can anyone advise what motivated woodpeckers to do this?

After a brief absence from the cabin during part of the holiday, we discovered a new dimension to the woodpecker. One had penetrated the cover on our stove chimney, negotiated a 10-foot trip down the chimney through an L-curve and the damper and threshed around in the cold firebox before climbing out again.

The kitchen looked like a disaster zone. Within an hour after we finished cleaning the place, a familiar rat-a-tat-tat sounded outside while my wife was napping.

When I returned from a walk, my bride was furious. She held a small round stone. ''What's that for?'' we asked, wondering what I had done wrong. ''I'm going to kill that blankety-blank bird,'' she said.

This story has a happy ending for birdlovers.

My wife couldn't hit a woodpecker with a shotgun, much less with a rock. This woodpecker, like the tax collector, will continue to be around.

So there's always next season. Hopefully, our feathered enemy will find another habitat. The area is full of trees, including many nice hollow ones, that would be easier and safer to penetrate.

We've covered all the holes in our attic, except the latest one, and we hope this lone woodpecker will die of boredom, or anti-boredom, if that's what it takes to get rid of woodpeckers.

WOODPECKERS: A MATTER OF SOME IMPORTANCE

One thing we have learned is that people are more concerned with woodpeckers than with the affairs of business and government.

The response to a column about our private war with woodpeckers was phenomenal, at least to a writer who considers two letters and a phone call to be an avalanche of fan response.

First, there was Joe Dealey, head of the corporation which owns and operates *The Dallas Morning News.*

"I see you have a woodpecker problem," Joe began by long distance telephone. I feared his next comment might be to quit using the valuable space in *The Dallas News* for airing my private difficulties.

"Let me tell you what we did down at Koon Kreek," Dealey continued. Then I knew we were on the same wave length.

Our leader then reported how he had nailed hardware cloth around the eaves of his house, and bought a plastic owl to frighten away the intruders. So far it has worked.

"And I hear Fred Pass has had all kinds of trouble with woodpeckers in his place at Cedar Creek," said Dealey. "He scared them away putting plastic snakes on the ledges."

Fred is an expert in rural problems. He has lived on the land much of his life, writes about it, and also edited the *Texas Almanac* while writing editorials. If anybody should know about woodpeckers, it is our friend from the tall pines of East Texas.

Unfortunately, we have neither plastic owl nor plastic snakes. We have a real hoot owl on our creek, but it never is around when woodpeckers are working on our cabin.

We also have snakes, poisonous and non-poisonous, and have killed two rattlers in the pumphouse. But our snakes likewise show little interest in woodpeckers. The only thing that's worked, short of open warfare, has been covering the holes in our attic with squares of tin. But the birds drill new holes faster than we can close them.

J. C. Dingwall, retired chief engineer of the State Highway Department, meditated aloud about the diamond-bit bills which woodpeckers possess. ''You'd think they'd beat their brains out pecking,'' said Dingwall. This may be a fact. Why else would a bird crawl down a hot chimney into the firebox of our wood stove?

And Chief Justice Joe R. Greenhill of the Texas Supreme Court delivered an opinion that woodpeckers are nearly everybody's problem. The chief justice seemed a little left out that woodpeckers are giving a friend's house fits while leaving the Greenhill home mostly alone.

Greenhill urged more woodpecker journalism. ''It takes courage to print a column like that,'' he remarked.

It takes something. We had such trepidation about the subject that we asked Executive Editor Tom Simmons whether he would print it. Simmons said yes, it would be a relief from the ballgames and politics.

WILD TURKEYS COMING BACK

On Thanksgiving morning the residents of Gravel Hill Ranch were excited to see three wild turkeys playing in the front yard.

It wasn't that they wanted these turkeys for dinner, as the Pilgrims did in days of yore.

The presence of wild turkeys on the Lampasas County ranch marked a major breakthrough in the growing and conservation of wild game on the land, once devastated by gun and plow, as well as overrun with varmints.

Once, we grew nine wild turkeys in the barn, starting with day-old poults furnished by a friend. After a few months, when the birds appeared large enough to fend for themselves, we turned the flock loose. Gradually, they disappeared, as do most wild turkeys reared in captivity. The survival rate of turkeys born in the wild is 20 times higher than for birds which are hatched in a barn and later released, according to wildlife experts.

After a year, we saw three turkey hens on the place and these occasionally roosted on the television antenna, safe from night-prowling predators, and — no kidding — improving TV reception.

But these too disappeared. One died on the highway, run over by a motor vehicle — among the greatest destroyers of wildlife. After two years, one hen remained. That summer the little grey-brown hen was badly mauled, apparently in a struggle to protect a nest from some wild animal or snake. For a long time, nobody saw any turkeys around, so we assumed all had been killed or drifted away to join another flock.

Then last summer, a hen showed up with two leggy young ones. Now they are at home on the range, so to speak, and to wild turkey lovers, it is a real thrill. Our Aggie grandson, home for the holidays, spotted them roosting in a tall dead tree along Donalson Creek.

The next morning I observed the big birds from a tree blind, scratching their way through the woods. Turkeys walk and run much more than they fly.

Hopefully, next spring will bring a new and larger hatch of the birds, although the odds of survival are still small.

What is happening here in Central Texas has occurred over nearly all the area native to wild turkeys in Texas. The landowners — yes, and hunters too — nearly all protect them carefully. Shooting wild turkeys on their nighttime roost, which reportedly was common in the old days, is now practically a hanging offense among conservationists, sportsmen, and ranchers.

Actually, parts of Central Texas are overstocked with deer. Wild turkeys will extend their range to new habitat when a flock gets large. Deer live and die within an area of five miles or less, and often will starve to death rather than move to more promising ground.

Not so with the wise turkey. A hen will travel up to 40 miles to mate and nest. If the first nest is destroyed, she will lay another nine or ten eggs and start over. In the same season, a turkey hen will make a third nest if the first two fail to produce surviving offspring.

Wild turkeys are bird-watching at its best. Thirty-five thousand Americans belong to the National Wild Turkey Federation, which publishes an interesting magazine title *Turkey Call*.

One issue contains an article by Levett E. Williams Jr., a

Florida wildlife biologist, who has been observing wild turkeys for 20 years, taking photographs and recording turkey talk. Williams reports that turkeys make more than 20 sounds, each with a special meaning.

The sound most often heard by a turkey hunter is ''putt' or ''putt putt'', which translates ''something is wrong here.'' When another turkey in the area ''putts'', it means ''Message received. I'm alert,'' according to Williams.

The call most often associated with the turkey by humans is the ''gobble'' or ''gobble gobble,'' sometimes followed by a gutteral purr. This says: ''I'm an adult male; come to me, hens, beware of other gobblers.'' Williams says to a hen this means ''My lover (maybe).'' To another gobbler it is a sign to clear out or get ready to fight for the lady's company.

The two calls most commonly imitated by man seeking to ''call up'' a gobbler are, according to Williams, the ''lost'' call and the plain yelp. The ''lost'' call helps summon a scattered flock together, and the plain yelp indicates another turkey is around, even if it is some fellow in a camouflage suit.

But the way things have been progressing in Texas in recent years, life for the wild turkey will get better. Fifty years ago, turkeys had disappeared from most of Texas. Now they are back in most of the original habitat—about 400,000 strong, the experts estimate.

NATURE CAN BE ROUGH

Bees in the attic are our latest problem.

These are not the wild, man-killing attack bees, apparently. They appear to be the domestic variety, who came from somewhere and decided to take up housekeeping beneath the corrugated tin roof of our cabin in the Lampasas country.

Bees make a nice sound, if you like buzzing. A few ventured indoors during our absence. They were found dead in the shower stall where they apparently sought water in vain.

The hive, if that's what it is, must be in one corner of the attic, because underneath this spot is the faint aroma of honey, a rather nice odor. Bees outside the house come and go beneath rippled eaves of the roof. The buzzing stops in the evening, and it resumes every morning at daybreak, when the dawn patrols take off in search of nectar.

It's a fascinating sight and sound, one bee after the other. Never before did I realize the full meaning of a "bee line." It means arrow-straight in one direction.

Many wildflowers still bloom and the agaritas are loaded red-ripe. There is clover in the fields, and bees love clover blossoms.

Unlike our woodpecker visitors, we may get accustomed to the bees, if our mutual housing project remains peaceful. Domestic bees won't sting, I'm told, unless they are disturbed. So we give them a good leaving alone, except to observe from a respectful distance.

If these bees are "tame" they must come from a nearby hive. But the gravel hill country has raised bees since long before the white man arrived 150 years ago. An enormous abandoned hive hangs high in a large live oak beside a small creek.

A more recent hive of wild bees inhabited a hollow tree until a 20-foot rise on Donalson Creek flooded the entrance a few years ago. The bees must have drowned, for we never saw them again.

Nature is wonderful, but nature also can be wild and cruel.

A female peacock setting on six eggs in the barn recently lost five eggs in one night to a predator, probably a snake. The sixth egg is infertile, showing the predator sought the unhatched birds.

Snakes help the ecological balance by catching rats and mice. But they also can play havoc with domestic fowl. One recently killed two pigeon squabs and a grown bird in a cage. All were too large for the snake to swallow. The reptile was captured by a 16-year-old grandson and carried to a remote pasture, a fate better than it deserved.

Also, the remainder of our small wild turkey flock has run into trouble from wild enemies. A turkey hen setting on a clutch of eggs in a nearby field was robbed by a predator, this one probably an animal such as opossum or raccoon. The hen suffered a bite on her leg trying to defend the nest, and she also lost most of her tail feathers along with the eggs.

Such incidents make up the "natural" world that many humans envy, often without knowing the whole facts. Outdoors and rural life are great, but it is far from all peace and gentleness. Nature can be as rough as it is beautiful.

Just as the wild plum tree may harbor a red wasp nest with its fine fruit, or even a rattlesnake nearby, the world of nature grows thorns as well as flowers.

Yet it is the real world, the very best there is. "Civilization" is really only a man-made veneer. It will never replace the natural world, nor should it. Birds, animals, and plants live and die, like humans, but life goes on with or without the "protection" of man.

When humans leave nature alone even for a few days, the bees and the woodpeckers may take over. They may not like living indoors as a regular thing. Being migratory, the woodpeckers flew away to return next fall. They left two more holes in our ancient board siding, one in the attic and another on a screened porch.

We patched three holes in the cabin last winter with pieces of tin in our losing bout with the flickers, but they were still ahead when spring arrived. We are not giving up. Neither will the hardy woodpeckers. Next time, we hope they won't mind sharing an attic with the bees.

OUT ON THE RURAL ROUTES

As a good many city folks are discovering, country living refreshes the soul, whether it comes as a weekend visit or a permanent residence. In a time when so many city people seem frustrated and discontented over high prices, faulty service, boredom, and political controversy, farmers and ranchers have found a silver lining. It comes in the form of higher prices for their products.

Prices at grocery stores have been rising for years, but very little of the increase heretofore trickled down to the man and his wife who have been milking the cows, tilling the soil, worming the calves, and trying to keep varmints from eating up the baby chicks. Mostly, the young folks left for city jobs.

Today, there's a real profit incentive for raising crops and livestock, although one still can't pay the prevailing prices for land and expect to pay it out of agricultural profits. The crop- and livestock-raiser simply cannot compete with the city investor in buying rural land.

There is happiness abroad in the country, however.

City workers by the thousands are moving to smaller towns or acreage, from where they commute to work. One change has been to provide some home-grown groceries, which develops in these citizens a greater appreciation for the risk, effort, and expense of growing food.

''The most expensive tomatoes ever grown'' is often the proud remark of a home gardener displaying his first crop.

The movement back to the land will have sociological and even political effects which may far outweigh the economic benefits. On the whole, rural citizens are friendlier, more concerned about each other, and more philosophical. Some may gossip, but generally they do care about others.

The late Gene Howe, Amarillo editor and columnist, once wrote that citizens of the Panhandle-Plains during the ''Dust Bowl'' days of the 1930s could ''make a living taking in each other's washing.''

Thankfully, times are better now; although we regret that hardly anybody can be hired today to do the family's washing.

Spring is generally regarded as the season of rising hope. But autumn is our favorite. The heat and irritations of the summer are over. Families settle into schedules attuned to school and work, spliced with large offerings of recreation and entertainment.

We liked summer better when school started after Labor Day, rather than in mid-August. In these days when public schools have become child-care institutions rather than mainly for education, most parents seem delighted to get their children out of the house.

Does any school system still stop classes during cotton-picking time so students can help gather the crop? Once that was the custom over much of Texas in the days when the "work ethic" was more widespread.

We regret that everybody can't enjoy a taste of rural life today, particularly youngsters who merely exist in the cities.

WEST TEXANS KNEW IT ALREADY

Chemists at the National Bureau of Standards are just discovering that air-borne sand has certain beneficial value — a fact learned long ago by West Texans.

The Bureau reports that ordinary sand will help soak up the spray-can gases which are said to threaten the earth's ozone layer.

Since ours is a spray-can civilization we can be thankful there is enough sand for our protection, as any Texan could have told you.

Swept by hurricane-force winds, and pure rich dirt from Arizona, New Mexico and West Texas fumigated the atmosphere up to about 10,000 feet, pilots say.

This made some people uneasy, such as Secretary of State Mark White, who was trying to fly back from Beaumont to Austin in a small airplane and noticed a truck on the ground was gaining on the aircraft.

West Texans never learn to love sandstorms but to tolerate them. Between dusters, the weather is usually beautiful to behold. What once were called "black blizzards" redistribute a lot of real estate in a hurry.

The late Gene Howe, editor of the *Amarillo News*, always insisted that duststorms contained "Vitamin K", which made West Texans more durable than ordinary people. We don't know if the biochemists ever came up with a scientific brand of "Vitamin K." West Texans viewed it as something akin to getting grit in one's craw, which every poultry raiser knows is essential to life and the pursuit of happiness.

During the Depression and the Dust Bowl days of the 1930s, West Texans who toughed it out rather than move to

California were bolstered by encouraging words of columnist Howe. He always insisted that the Texas plains are the only place in the world "where everybody can make a living taking in each other's washing."

Social planners should think this over.

Howe also contended "Vitamin K" and other ingredients of blowing soil not only clear the ozone of impurities, but give those inhaling it special powers.

For instance, Howe claimed most West Texans got so adept at catching jackrabbits to eat during the 1930s the hunter would run alongside the rabbit to feel if he was fat before capturing his meal. Jackrabbits then were called "Hoover hams," since the Democrats in those days blamed all the nation's troubles on the Republican Administration, which they managed to do successfully for many years thereafter.

Air conditioning was practically non-existent and buildings much more open to outside air in those days; so duststorms sometimes invaded the state capitol, causing legislators to wear gauze masks like those used in operating rooms.

When things improved and even air conditioning was available on automobiles, we remember an old-timer near Lubbock, who bought a new car but did not install air conditioning. He was so embarrassed at this poverty that he rode around even in the hottest weather with the windows rolled up, so his friends couldn't know he wasn't air conditioned.

But the old-timer developed a problem. He chewed tobacco and often forgot to roll down the window.

COW RUSTLING STILL AROUND

A young couple we know, getting started in the cattle business, returned home recently from an overnight trip to discover a 1,000-pound yearling bull missing from a pasture.

The animal, valued at $1,000 for future breeding purposes, could have wound up in some thief's freezer or on sale over the counter of a distant butcher shop.

Cattle rustling is as old as livestock ranching, and thieves are just as active now as during the bad old days, according to

Secretary-General Manager Don King of the Texas and Southwestern Cattle Raisers Association headquartered in Fort Worth.

The association was started in 1876 in an effort to combat theft of livestock and equipment.

Losses run to thousands of dollars per day, including saddles, trailers, and equipment as well as livestock. It is worst around big cities such as Dallas and Houston. Ironically, livestock-growing flourishes even close to the cities, and so does rustling.

King believes one reason for such crime is the leniency of urban courts and juries in livestock stealing, whereas rural juries are more likely to view the matter as a major crime rather than mere property loss.

Both rustling operations and detective work of field inspectors for the association are increasingly sophisticated. Most thieves "know livestock" and how to handle the big animals, said King. After all, it isn't easy for an amateur to load a 1,000-pound or larger animal into a truck.

Some modern rustlers operate with hoist trucks. They shoot the animal and load the carcass into the truck. This has not appeared yet in Texas, said King, but in some states livestock thieves travel in trucks equipped for full butchering operations.

Conviction of livestock theft carries a 2- to 10-year sentence, and fence cutting is a 2- to 5-year penalty, if the court wants to assess it.

Especially tragic to owners and the livestock industry is the theft of high-grade breeding animals worth thousands of dollars, which may be butchered by thieves for the meat. A few are shot in the pasture and only the hind quarters carried off, leaving the remainder for varmints and buzzards. This violation occurs most frequently during the fall hunting season, King said.

In many years with the association, King said he sees little relationship between the price of beef and rustling activity. It is an ever-present problem.

Professional rustlers are more likely to steal a truckload of livestock than one or two animals. The risk is just as great with a smaller number and the reward much smaller.

"Bad neighbors" often steal one or two animals at a time, by letting the fence down or picking the cattle out of a pasture in the area.

About 90 brand inspectors for Texas and Southwestern Cattle Raisers Association scrutinize animals sold weekly through Texas' 180 auctions. Most thieves are smart enough to avoid the auction with branded livestock.

King said a typical rustler knows the territory and watches stock feeding schedules so he can strike when the rancher's back is turned.

Some tips from King on protecting livestock from theft:

Avoid building pens beside a road, and keep loading chutes chained and locked.

Lock all outside gates. Any evidence of a tampered-with lock raises the rancher's suspicion immediately and brings early reporting of thefts.

Vary stock-feeding schedules so the prospective thief can't be sure when you are coming.

Report losses promptly to local officers and the cattle raisers association, which helps non-members, too.

"We want to get these people out of circulation," King explained about rustlers.

PEACOCKS FOR FATHER'S DAY

For Father's Day the gift I received was a pair of grown peacocks.

A quick poll of the Ol' Fitz (drinking) Club at the Austin Headliners' Club reveals this may be the most unique Father's Day remembrance of anyone in my acquaintance.

Our daughter's family, living in Lampasas County, arranged for the gift. Understandably, it cost them nothing, for their friend who owned peacocks had an oversupply. This is easy to achieve.

Two peacocks may be too many. Mine were delivered separately in "tow sacks," the burlap bags once containing livestock and poultry feed. The dictionary says "gunny" is a synonym for burlap, and that "tow" is a rough fiber from flax or hemp. Most such sacks are made from hemp.

Our peacocks are housed temporarily in a shed used last year for growing wild turkeys, most of which disappeared when released.

The worst trait of the peacock is its ungodly scream, usually at dawn or dusk, or any time the fancy strikes one. The peacock cries like a wounded banshee, or like running your mother-in-law through a wringer.

The peacock can be heard for miles, and if the listener doesn't know the sound, it is likely to be mistaken for humans being tortured.

Nobody needs an alarm clock to wake up in our country any more. The peacocks do that.

Our experience with the regal bird is limited. The male is resplendent, with tail feathers at least four feet long, and beautifully marked in blues, greens, and golds. By comparison, the peahen (or shall we call her peaperson) is drab. The hen's face looks like paint, plus a cute little topknot feather.

Peacocks, like the noisy guinea, are known mostly in this country for their ability to provide early warning systems for persons engaged in such illicit activities as making moonshine whiskey. If friend or foe approaches the site, a din of sound rises. They also are said to keep snakes away.

In Europe, during the heyday of kings and princes, the peacock decorated the grounds of castles and estates. It also was coveted as food. King Ludwig the Mad of Bavaria, noted for spending his subjects' taxes building magnificent castles, was a peacock fancier. Whenever Ludwig wanted a feast, he had peacocks roasted for the main dish.

We can attest to the excellence of King Ludwig's taste.

Late one evening while hunting deer in the Hill Country of Texas, I saw a flock of turkey hens winding down the hill headed for the roost. One was a strange looking bird. I knew it wasn't a turkey, and shot it thinking it some kind of a freak.

It was after dark when I reached camp with the bird, and my companions debated what I had bagged. Most thought it was a hybrid of turkey and peacock, although the landowner said no peacocks had been in the area for years. My companions called it a "peakie" or "turcock." Only our Mexican cook, Cruz, knew the true identity of the bird.

Cruz also cooked the bird for lunch the next day, and she was delicious, tasting like a large pheasant.

Later, we learned from University of Texas biologists that peacocks and turkeys cannot cross-breed.

We are going to release my Father's Day gift just as soon as they get acquainted with their new home.

CHIGGER CONTROL

The U.S. government has a program which will benefit us. It is "Controlling Chiggers."

This is the title of a U.S. Department of Agriculture bulletin offered free of charge to each "patron," compliments of Uncle Sam and Congressman Jake Pickle, and delivered by the postmen.

As soon as we can pick out nine other bulletins, among about 100 offered, an order will go straight to Washington.

Chiggers, sometimes called redbugs, have a personal meaning for us. On the calf of our left leg at this very moment rises an irritating red bump. We blame this on a chigger, who evaded the insect repellant sprayed on our pants cuff the last time we took to the tall grass.

We have never really seen a chigger, but will testify they are alive and hungry, despite the drouth.

As a taxpayer who feels he is supporting both the old and the young, the rich and the poor, we have long felt that the federal government offers us little except the opportunity to pay more taxes and receive more trash mail.

The offer of a free chigger control booklet has improved Washington's image with us, at a time when our opinion of government needs an uplift.

Choosing nine more pamphlets raises a challenge for making decisions that tax our brain (which is about all there is left untaxed).

There's one on ''Control of Bedbugs,'' which hopefully we can skip right now.

Leaflet L 501 deals with ''The Old House Borer,'' which could be the title of our autobiography.

L 445 provides information on ''Electric Heating of Hotbeds,'' which sounds redundant as well as way out of season.

Many of these handy guides deal with ''how to buy . . .'' various foods. A separate title discusses ''how to get your money's worth in foods.''

GG 77 covers ''Family Food Stockpile for Survival.'' Several people we know maintain well-stocked fallout shelters, whose provisions may be well-aged by now if they haven't drunk it. We have had a Christmas fruitcake in our freezer for three years now. There is a bulletin on ''freezing meat and fish in the home'' but nothing on frozen fruitcake.

Awhile back we could have used F 2202 ''Simple plumbing Repairs for the Home and Farmstead,'' but this instruction comes too late. We gave up plumbing after trying to replace the screw-on rubber float in our toilet tank. By the time we abandoned this ''simple Plumbing Repair,'' the bathroom was awash. A plumber fixed it in 10 minutes.

The last publication offered by USDA and Congressman Pickle in the latest mailing is AH. 38 — ''First Aid for Flooded Homes and Farms.''

Right now we have more need for an effective bulletin on

how to do the rain dance. It is dry, dry, dry in Central Texas, and we wish our congressman would do something about that, Jake.

THE TEXAS WILDFLOWER MAN

While thousands of Texans enjoy the spring wildflowers, Carroll Abbott views nature's beauty with more serious purpose. Abbott collects and sells wildflower seeds and plants. He isn't getting rich at it, but leads a satisfying and often eventful life.

Once a highway patrol car drove slowly along the roadside where Abbott on all-fours was busy scratching the grass and putting his catch in a brown paper bag. In a few minutes, the patrol car cruised back again with its red light flashing. The officer asked what Abbott was doing.

''Collecting gaillardia pulchella,'' replied Abbott. The patrolman allowed that Abbott shouldn't get smart with him, possibly suspecting a marijuana freak.

''Indian blanket wildflower seed,'' Abbott explained. ''Some call it firewheel.''

''It's against the law to pick wildflowers along the highway,'' the patrolman continued.

''Yep, I know it, but if you arrest me you'll have to issue a ticket to every person you see gathering pecans or anything along the right-of-way. They're all seeds. You're asking for a mess of trouble.'' The patrolman drove off, shaking his head.

Abbott had other brushes with the law while pursuing his hobby-business, but always emerged triumphant by explaining that he is just trying to preserve wildflowers and spread their beauty. He carries literature to support his story, including price lists for seed and plants sold mostly by mail through his firm name ''Green Horizons'' in Austin.

Although many other states have commercial wildflower and wild plant distributors, Abbott believes he is the only Texan operating on a statewide basis.

A sometimes-employee of the State Democratic Party in Texas, sometimes-Kerrville newspaper publisher, one-time publisher of a magazine devoted entirely to longhorn cattle, Abbott is an unconventional nature lover. After all, one man's wildflower often is another man's weed.

Abbott travels about 50,000 miles a year, looking for plants where seed may be gathered later. One frustration is that highway department roadside mowing machines often trim the flowers before they seed. He has a running feud with highway officials about this, so far with negative results.

"The hazards are numerous and the heartbreaks are often," says Abbott. "Many, many times, a mother-plant has been eaten by a cow, dug up by an armadillo, stomped under by a horse, mowed down by a farmer who forgot we were coming back, burned off in a brush fire — or worse still, picked clean while in bloom by a thoughtless lover of beauty."

Texas is blessed with more than 5,000 varieties of wildflowers and plants, and Abbott is able to collect only a few hundred for seed and plants. Abbott says Texas is particularly fortunate in the variety of wildflowers and plants that are ornamental for yard and other decoration. Some seed are so tiny they are merely dust. A pinch equals 200 to 500 seeds, and these require special planting.

A sort of Johnny Appleseed of Texas wildlife, Abbott enjoys his work.

REMEMBER THE PET ROCK CRAZE?

The demand for rock pets, or pet rocks, was one of the more fascinating developments of a Christmas season now passed.

We tried to decide how to help disappointed readers whose Santa stocking did not include a rock pet. This is a really brilliant idea, for such pets do not need to be fed, watered, vaccinated, or taken to the bathroom, but furnish a lifetime of pleasure in return for tender loving care.

Establishment of Gravel Hill Rock Pet Foundation Uninc. seems to be the answer to helping persons wishing one of these durable little housebroken friends. Rocks are one thing that Gravel Hill Ranch has plenty of.

These are wild rocks with centuries of history behind them. They have been carefully cultivated by generations of people seeking to upset the rock habitat and make it grow more civilized products such as grass, sorghum, cotton, or even gardens. This disturbs the environment.

Many of these rocks would have been oil-rich, but for the fact in prehistoric eras, the rocks from Gravel Hill's bed of marine fossils tilted upward and the petroleum ran down beneath the Gulf of Mexico to be captured and burned and often wasted eons later by men and women lacking sympathy for their rock heritage.

The rocks remaining at Gravel Hill are poor but proud, although many retain markings of their rich ancestors, such as huge fossilized snails and oyster shells.

These rocks long predate recorded history, and were old, old before Jesus Christ was born in Bethlehem. As rock pets go, the signers of the Declaration of Independence at Philadelphia years ago are Johnnies-come-lately.

Although even wild rocks are normally quite docile, outside agitators have been known to cause damage, injury, and even death by careless direction of rocks. To get along well with such pets, one must think like a rock.

Rock pets are individual. They come in all colors and shapes, some shaggy rough and others so smooth-haired they feel more so than a Chihuahua. Some are so large they make a St. Bernard insignificant, and others so small that ants store them in holes beneath the ground.

We have a real feeling for rocks, having been reared on the plains where nothing but rich dirt covers the ground, and one had to dig down several feet to find a decent rock. This is no problem in Central Texas, where a rock is yours for the taking unless it happens to be somebody's diamond ring.

Rock hounds have been sniffing for rock pets, but the location of Gravel Hill is kept somewhat secret to prevent poaching. After all, the county commissioner hauled off tons of pet rocks to build a road for callous motorists who unfeelingly run over rocks that took millions of years to grow.

We have thought of letting Gravel Hill Rock Pet Foundation distribute rock pets to unfortunate readers who would like to adopt a rock but do not know how to go about it.

Right now, we are stymied by the financial and tax angles of getting rock pets to deserving people. How much would the post office people charge to deliver a pet rock? Since these rock pets are first class, the travel expense might be as enormous as sending a *Dallas News* reporter to New Orleans.

Also, there's Bob Bullock and the sales tax angle. Even though, our foundation would be non-profit, as are our other enterprises, just as surely as we accepted money from anybody in return for delivering a rock pet in Texas, Bullock's Raiders from the Comptroller's Department would come riding over the hill, if they could find it.

Of course, the foundation could declare bankruptcy, which it already is. And Mr. Bullock would have to be satisfied selling rock pets at auction to satisfy his ego. And he just might sell enough to pay off the national debt.

OWNING A DOG, AND VICE VERSA

For a few days I owned half a dog. George Slaughter owned the other half, although at one point it appeared the dog owned George.

The whole dog went to Tom Waddell, our longtime friend and waterfowl expert at Eagle Lake. A 3-month-old golden retriever named Waddell's Smokey in the American Kennel Club registry, Smokey's pedigree reaches from Georgia to Great Britain, and probably back to Runnymede.

You could tell right away Smokey was no ordinary pooch. The largest male in a litter of eight, he temporarily bore the name of Monster Man. The breeder must have been a football fan.

It had been years since I owned a dog, and it was pleasant to have an interest in Waddell's Smokey-Monster Man even for a few days. Our last dog was a fox terrier named Spot, who tackled a milk truck. That was the end of Spot. We went into cats after Spot was rubbed out.

A dog came back into my life because Waddell's last remaining golden retriever, old Dusty, just doesn't care much about hunting anymore. Waiting beside an icy pond to retrieve a dead duck is no longer Dusty's idea of having a good time. One winter, Waddell told us he is getting too old to train another dog. George and I asked again.

"That'd be fine," chirped Tom at the suggestion we bring him a new dog.

With the aid of Ginger Gotcher, a lively young woman who heads the Austin Golden Retriever Club, we found a suitable pup, Ginger owns the sire, a championship retriever, and the mother dog likewise bears aristocratic bloodlines.

Ginger met us at the suburban home of Dr. and Mrs. Fred Wilbur, where the mother dog and puppies romped around the shady back yard. Ginger had agreed to choose a hunting dog for us.

First, she separated three male pups from five females. Next she tossed out a deceased feathered pigeon, which is stored in her Deepfreeze for such purpose. Monster Man-Smokey bounded straight for the bird, picked it up carefully in his mouth and returned it to Ginger, while the other two pups just acted surprised.

"Here's your hunting dog," said Ginger. Then she examined him, especially head and mouth, and pronounced the puppy a winner.

How do you train a dog, especially as one as lovable as this?

"I'm strict on them," said Ginger. "If you want a pet, that's different. But a good dog must be disciplined."

She also lets the dog know when he does it right.

Two weeks later, Monster Man-Smokey and I were riding with George in his truck headed for Eagle Lake. The pup howled for a few minutes until we let him out of the carrying crate. The remainder of the trip, he rode happily up front with us.

After an hour, the puppy climbed in George's lap and fell asleep. I offered to remove the pup from the driver's lap. "Oh, he's all right," said George. "You know, I think I'll keep this pup and we'll get Tom another one."

Then George remembered his family already had four dogs, including one transient, and he decided even a Golden

Retriever would be too much to add.

George related a relative's experience training a dog. After considerable effort, this one learned to bring the morning newspaper from the lawn onto the front porch. This was fine, until the morning they found 17 newspapers piled on the porch.

As we drove up to Tom's white frame home, he came to the back gate to greet us and introduced himself to Smokey, whose name he'd already selected. Dusty sniffed around his new yard-mate for a few minutes, then decided the newcomer was all right.

Since Tom's mouth was hurting from the extraction of four teeth the day before, he excused himself from going to lunch. But he obviously was a happy man, with a new bright interest in life.

"Smokey won't be ready for the teal season in September," Tom announced as we prepared to leave. "He'll be ready for the big season in November."

A few days later, Waddell wrote that Smokey "never whined . . . made it perfect."

"He is a natural," Tom continued. "Won't need much training . . . just show him what I expect. He knows the yard and flower bed are his so he is satisfied. We will get along."

The letter concluded: "Hope we can both watch him when the goose and duck season open this year."

We hoped so too. There's no more thrilling sight than to watch the great flocks come off the roosting ponds at daybreak on the Lissie Prairie, headed for breakfast in the rice fields. Smokey will love it too.

TWO OLD FRIENDS IN DOG HEAVEN

Inside the letter was a snapshot of a gray-muzzled Golden Retriever. On the back was written. "Roger May 1962. June 5, 1977. Taken one week before he died. An all-time perfect retriever." It was like losing an old friend, but a flood of happy memories came.

Roger was the favorite dog of a friend, Tom T. Waddell of Eagle Lake, himself an old-timer. So many times I had enjoyed the company of Tom and Roger.

We would drive in the pre-dawn blackness to the Lissie Prairie in the back of Tom's ranch vehicle. The hunters and Roger then slogged through the wet grass in a pasture to the pond where decoys bobbed in the wind.

On Tom's command, Roger laid beside the pit where the hunters were concealed, until ducks or geese came within range. Then Roger would hit the water or gallop across the field for a downed bird. Roger never missed a duck or a goose, and when a hunter did, one could read disgust on Roger's face even in dim light.

It was a grand sight to watch Roger trot back with a goose held high. Tom boasted that Roger never lost a cripple.

In the last few hunts near Eagle Lake, most of the heavy work fell to Dusty, a younger golden retriever. We liked Dusty too, but there'll never be another Roger, a classic waterfowl dog. Dusty lacked some of Roger's obedience, but he was just as eager to go.

On one hunt, Tom decided to leave Roger in his pen. It was heartbreaking to watch.

"It's the first hunt Roger missed with me since I got him," Tom said as we drove away. Dusty was thumping around the back, raring to go.

Roger was not only old. He was nearly blind and deaf. Fifteen is old age for a dog. On his last hunt before being retired, Roger was so feeble he would stand in the pond waiting for a bird to fall, so he could beat Dusty to the game. Roger was a born retriever, and a great one.

The love of a sportsman for his hunting dog is a joy to behold. There's a special affection between a veteran hunter and his old dog who has given long and faithful service.

Joe Lanham's Old Bill is another example.

Joe, a former SMU football player, practices law here to support his habit of quail hunting. Joe raised pointers for pleasure. Old Bill was his favorite, and we had the honor of accompanying them a couple of years in the Hill Country.

Joe called Bill "Old Folks."

There were younger, more active dogs than Old Bill on the

hunt but none surpassed his quail sense. Once Old Bill, then weak of eyes and ears, scented quail in a clump of brambles alongside a creek. Two dogs had missed them, but Old Bill went rigid to the point. We flushed the covey and got three.

Another time, a wounded quail ran into a hole beneath a cedar tree. It was rattlesnake country where I wouldn't have stuck my hand in a hole for a hundred dollars. But Old Bill began digging furiously and came out proudly with a dusty quail.

One fall, when we were getting ready to hunt again, Lanham reported sadly, "I lost Old Bill."

Old Bill was literally lost. He was hunting in the South Texas brush country, making a sweep in search of birds, and was never found again. Joe and his partners looked everywhere for Bill, who must have dropped dead in a remote place. For Bill would have come to the whistle, if he was still alive.

There surely is a dog heaven for friends like Roger and Old Bill. It was great to make them part of my life and memory.

TEXANS TAKING TO THE WOODS

A "rich Texan" we know (actually a self-made millionaire from Minnesota) was asked how he managed to possess a showplace livestock farm in Northeast Texas.

"It's easy," he replied. "All it took was 10 years of hard work, plus a million dollars."

The owner added that the place still isn't showing a profit, despite tax loss write-offs.

Over much of Texas, "town money" is buying rural land at prices which are prohibitive to those trying to earn a living from farming and livestock. Most of the new owners, however, are far from rich. They are just fed up with the cities.

A University of Texas faculty member, noted for outspoken advice on running the University and the country, purchased a few acres on a cedar-covered "mountain" top in Central Texas. His students were shocked when he added the admonition: "And I'll kill anybody who trespasses."

Over the eastern half of Texas, particularly, dilapidated farm buildings and undernourished over-farmed cropland are being restored by new owners seeking escape from the concrete jungles, with their increasing problems of pollution, crime, and traffic.

One must get off the expressways to discover what is really happening, for the new city-bred farmer-stockmen prefer land along the back roads and houses distant from the front gate.

Old houses and cabins are preferred by the do-it-yourself types who spend weekends and vacations making like pioneers. Magnificent old plantation homes, neglected and often vacant for years, are coming alive again with new roofs and windows and gleaming paint.

The mobile home and pickup-camper are favored rural lodging for thousands who earn salaries in towns and cities to spend increasingly in getting back to the soil.

Industry management, of course, already has noticed this trend and is helping it along by locating new plants near small towns, where workers can most easily divide time between a wage-earning job and independent agriculture. Perhaps one-fourth of the vehicles parked in the employee spaces around the state capitol are pickup trucks.

The 3- and 4-day week for industrial workers has significant implications for government, which we feel the forecasters may be missing. Rural schools, mostly on the downgrade or disappeared, may be in demand again in a few years. Otherwise, increasing numbers of rural children must be bused to town schools.

The irritating problems of racial desegregation in public schools are hastening the exodus to rural residences of young families with school-age children.

Property values and school enrollment are skyrocketing, for example, in Leander ISD, about 25 miles northwest of Austin as this city struggles with its desegregation and other problems. Previously, Leander remained almost a ghost village. Now it has a real estate development plus a new schoolhouse.

THE PROBLEM WITH GRASS . . .

An eminent jurist we know was horrified to learn his wife had permitted some young apartment dwellers in the neighborhood to plant a garden on their vacant lot.

His honor had visions of marijuana springing up all over the place, with attendant headlines such as ''pot patch found on high court judge's lot.''

As it turned out, whatever the young people planted withered and died in the drouth and the judicial couple never did find out if their anxiety was justified.

This is by way of introduction to our spotty experience in grass culture.

Our small front flower garden (in the University of Texas neighborhood) has just sprouted a mysterious slender plant which my suspicious wife thinks might have been planted by a marijuana smoker. Personally, I think it is a weed; but that's what many people call tobacco.

We have asked several persons, mostly student types, if they can identify the plant, and they profess complete ignorance of marijuana. So does a Mexican-American friend. The responses couldn't be more guarded if we worked for the Bureau of Narcotics and Dangerous Drugs and were trying to pin a rap on them.

Hopefully, the strange plant will be easier to exterminate than the bermuda grass which grows between the flagstones of the front walk. We have pulled the stuff repeatedly, cut it off, dug it up, salted it with the brine from homemade ice cream, poured on gasoline and weed killer.

Right now, we have a healthy looking crop of bermuda grass in our front walk (despite having the cracks concreted), the plants are seeding, and look like they will multiply where we have for years tried to replace the Bermuda with St. Augustine.

Grass-growing on a recently acquired farm has been just as frustrating. In our scientific manner, we planted commercial pasture grass seed in one plot which can be watered. This experimental grass plot was cultivated carefully.

So far, it has produced the most abundant combination of weeds in the history of horticulture, including a combination of sandburrs, thistles, and wild grass types, which even hungry livestock ignores. One place with a good stand of grass is under a wire fence where cultivation is impossible.

On another plot, refined pasture grass was planted last October. If it has come up yet, nobody can identify it. This possibly is the result of assorted weeds and undesirable plants, mostly sharp pointed, which possess this fertile acreage. Included are robust specimens of johnson grass, which we don't blame on the former president from Stonewall.

One success can be reported. Buffalo grass is coming along well in one place we planted. This is in tracks left by a bulldozer.

FOR AND AGAINST — EAGLES

As the politicians say, there are two sides to the eagle question. Some of my friends favor the eagle, and some of my friends are against it. I am for my friends.

Gov. Dolph Briscoe put on one of his better performances for the press, defending ranchers who want to get rid of some golden eagles. The big predatory birds of Southwest Texas "murder innocent, helpless, defenseless, little lambs and kids (goats)," said Briscoe. He had just asked the federal government to relax its prohibition on killing golden eagles in the interest of saving young livestock from birds of prey.

Briscoe knows from experience what an eagle can do. He raises sheep and goats, and so do his neighbors.

The conservationists have a point also. The bald eagle, our national bird, has dwindled to small numbers in the northern United States and the southern peninsula of Alaska. Frankly, we wonder why our forefathers selected a predatory bird as the national symbol. But the eagle is wild and free and strong. That's one reason its detractors dislike the eagle.

What this country needs is balance, ecological and otherwise. It isn't difficult to get overstocked on eagles, or coyotes, or opossums, or rattlesnakes, or raccoons, or hawks, to name a few from our experiences. Extermination isn't the answer, but control is.

This is a more or less civilized country, and the old law of fang and claw is out of place. Shooting eagles from airplanes must be controlled, just as the depredations of eagles must be controlled.

All predators, including eagles, are killers. A dainty young lady whom we know grew up on a ranch in the eagle country of Val Verde County. Once her father brought a crippled young eagle home. It had fallen from the nest and broken a wing. The family kept the eagle in a big cage while it healed, feeding it raw meat. It didn't like dead meat but preferred live fare like rabbits.

When the eagle was nearly grown, it was put on a large screened porch one time while the family went to town. When they got back, two pet doves had been eaten and the family dog was scared half to death. The eagle was released, and presumably lived happily ever afterward.

A 15-year-old ranch lad in the Lampasas country attributes the loss of some prized homing pigeons to hawks which nest on the place, and he has helped protect them. Hawks also eat rabbits, mice, and snakes, but they'd just as soon eat your chickens. A hawk can become a daily killer of grown chickens.

Eagles, of course, kill larger animals. We once heard testimony by a West Texas rancher who had witnessed the slaughter of a 6-point-buck by an eagle, dive-bombing the sizable deer on the neck until he fell and was killed with talons and beak.

Some zoologists disagree, saying eagles are too small to kill healthy livestock. But the evidence is strong on the other side. Also, persons from eagle country say the big birds prefer killing their meat, rather than dining on carcasses of already-dead animals. Since the golden eagle and the buzzard, which eats only dead or dying animals, are similar, it is possible the buzzard is sometimes mistaken for an eagle. Except in flight, it is difficult to tell the birds apart.

Coyotes are a costly menace to domestic and wildlife through much of Texas, since cyanide poisoning has been banned except in special cases. In some counties, ranchers have given up trying to rear young sheep and goats because of the predators.

Coyotes serve a useful purpose in controlling overpopulation by rabbits, mice, and other smaller animals, but the cunning coyote certainly isn't all good. He is a killer, very adaptable to populated areas, and even eats your finest melons.

Persons who feel the farmer and rancher isn't interested in protecting endangered species are mistaken. The most dedicated, practical conservationists I know live on the land and love it.

But the struggle between man and nature is unrelenting. Wisdom and understanding are necessary to persons of differing viewpoints — including control over the eagle on the livestock ranges of Southwest Texas.

SHOOTING SNAKES

One summer afternoon while we sat on the south front porch of the cabin at Gravel Hill, admiring the fields and hills, our granddaughter Laura exclaimed:

"There's a copperhead!"

"A what?," I responded, awakened from pleasant reverie.

"A copperhead . . . a snake."

"Where is there any copperhead?"

"Right there on the walk, coming toward the steps."

Grandson Curtis had already bolted into the house, and he came back with a shotgun and two shells.

Deferentially, he handed the firearm to me although Curtis, a member of the Texas A&M rifle team, is a much better shot.

"Which way is he pointed now?" asked nearsighted me. I did detect a brown and reddish movement in the grass between the flagstones, but couldn't discern whether it was coming or going.

"He's coming this way," I was told.

So I fired at the middle of the intruder, hoping to stop it — going or coming. Limestone dust flew and the snake retreated down the walk, wounded but extremely dangerous. A copperhead is the only snake that will seek out a human just to inject its poison although rattlesnakes and cottonmouth water moccasins will bite if you cross them.

The copperhead moved to the end of the flagstone walk, curled to strike, but the next shot finished him.

This story is told mainly to illustrate that guns serve citizens in ways which the gun-hater mentality would never recognize.

Personally, I never have liked or trusted pistols. They are

the weapon of the criminal as well as the police, and even in friendly hands are much more dangerous than rifles or shotguns.

Any person who possesses a firearm should learn how to use it safely, for guns have been indispensable to survival in rural America for generations.

Even rattlesnakes serve a purpose, such as catching rats and mice, but humans must be careful in rattlesnake country, which covers most of the United States.

A visitor from Michigan was mightily impressed on this while leaving the ranch house to attend church in Lampasas. She was already at the car outside the yard when our daughter, reared in the city but living in the country, stepped back into the house and returned with a .410 gauge shotgun, which she fired into the flower bed beside the steps. She exterminated a sizable rattlesnake the Michigan lady had nearly stepped on.

This done, the ranch wife straightened her Sunday dress, replaced the shotgun inside the front door, and went serenely to church with her shaken in-law.

On another occasion, a town lad visiting the ranch expressed hope to see some of the real Wild West.

As the family and guest sat down to supper, a strange sound came from the back yard. Outside they saw a game of cat-and-rattlesnake. The family Persian was mesmerizing a rattlesnake, coiled and buzzing under the carport. The cat, almost a stranger to snakes, instinctively stayed outside the reptile's striking range. The snake was dispatched with a shotgun as the startled town boy watched. He took the 10 rattles from the snake as a souvenir of the visit.

When we acquired Gravel Hill several years ago, rattlesnakes and copperheads were plentiful, thanks partly to the long neglect of the premises that allowed poisonous snakes and black widow spiders to take over. You learn to watch where you step or put a hand.

One large rattlesnake was caught in a cage trap set to catch a family of skunks that had taken up residence in the little pump house beside our cabin.

The snake was very angry about his captivity. We also

caught one skunk and the others left. The skunk was released on another part of the ranch.

Days later, I opened the pumphouse door for a casual inspection and was horrified to find inside a large rattler, coiled, weaving and forking his tongue almost in my face. I dashed to the house for the trusty .16 gauge, loading it on the return. I blew the intruder and a piece of the door sill to pieces.

I must have said something special on this occasion.

"I never heard you use language like that," said my wife, refusing to repeat my remark. I don't know what I said but I couldn't have been more surprised had I found a rattlesnake in the refrigerator ready to strike.

NOTHING NEW WITH BUFFALO

Old-timers of the Texas Panhandle Plains were surprised in 1955 to hear Canadians claiming a scientific discovery of cattalo by crossing a cow with a buffalo.

The breed was developed on a sizable scale in Texas before 1905 by the late Col. Charles Goodnight, famed rancher of the North Panhandle Plains. Several modern Texans also are raising the crossbred animals.

The announcement that a cattalo had been produced in Alberta, Canada, was made at the International Genetics Congress in Montreal.

J. Evetts Haley of Canyon, well-known historian, recounts Goodnight's experience breeding and raising cattalo in his biography of the cattleman published in 1936 by Houghton Mifflin Company. Goodnight loved buffalo as well as cattle and for half a century kept both breeds on his ranches, principally near Palo Duro Canyon, east of Amarillo.

Goodnight found one cattalo calf loose on the range in 1883, Haley said. Two years later, the rancher started his experiments, breeding a buffalo bull to a Polled Angus beef cow.

Only female offsprings were born on the first cross, Haley reported. For some reason Goodnight never understood, all first-cross cattalo bulls died at birth. But the female cattalo were bred both to domestic bulls and buffalo bulls, with a large number of calves of both sexes.

A Polled Angus bull bred to half buffalo cows established a fertile strain that had grown to 40 head of cattalo by 1917.

Haley reported that the breed seemed immune to disease, particularly deadly blackleg. It gained weight faster than domestic cattle, grew larger, multiplied at much greater age, and produced tasty meat, the rancher said. The cattalo did not run from flies nor drift in storms. Neither were they ill-tempered, but ''were solicitous mothers.''

''They required less salt than common cattle, scarcely disturbed their waterings, and refused to eat loco (weed),'' Haley wrote. ''They had eight incisors, which enabled them to bite off the grass as low as a buffalo, and gave them the benefit of rich seeds in the tussets of the buffalo grass. Their meat had less fiber, was tenderer, and for some reason seemed easier to keep or cure than beef.''

Goodnight kept the cattalo on his ranch for many years, convinced the breed had a future. Others did not share his enthusiasm. The breed eventually developed an ailment that caused loss of calves by premature birth. Rather than continue the expensive experiment, Colonel Goodnight sold his cattalo herd.

Buffalo meat was still the old rancher's favorite food when he died at the age of 95.

Evetts Haley, a sturdy states righter in politics as well as a successful rancher and historian, gave this memory of his friend, Charles Goodnight:

''During 70 years of his mature life, he struggled with the problems of the open country, and liked it. Government subsidy for its people, and paternalistic removal to lands where life was comfortable and easy, would have galled his sensitive soul. He died in time. Of course the scientific world denied him, but we who recall our traditions in the shade of ranch corrals like to remember him as the Burbank and the philosopher of the open range.''

. . . WHERE THE BUFFALO ROAM

''Buffalo Bob'' Strauss' bison barbecue recipe is a myth.

That's according to his secretary, notwithstanding a burst of national publicity that then Ambassador Robert S. Strauss

35

and his wife, Helen, were barbecuing buffalo for 300 attending a White House party honoring dignitaries from Japan.

When word was broadcast that the Strausses could barbecue buffalo, we fired off a letter to our longtime friend from Stamford and Dallas, requesting a copy of the recipe. The Moreheads, husband and wife, have co-authored *Texas Wild Game Cook Book* and wished to include the Strauss recipe in the next edition.

We were saddened by the telephoned report from his girl Friday: ''Mr. Strauss has no recipe for buffalo barbecue. That report was greatly overblown in the media.'' Strauss did ''fix up something'' for the sauce, she explained, but it wasn't any recipe, just a few ingredients mixed together at the White House's request for something with a Texas flavor. As everyone knows, President Carter called on Strauss for everything from maintaining world peace to keeping the country prosperous.

Doubtless Strauss grew up on barbecue, coming from Stamford, Texas, a town noted for cattle and cowboys. In the ranch country, however, the natives will more likely order a good steak. We doubt Strauss would push buffalo (whose real name is bison) as table fare for foreigners because the former U.S. trade envoy is trying to sell our overseas friends on eating beef, which is a more plentiful product than buffalo meat.

But buffalo are edible, and considered tasty as well as nutritious. Early plainsmen slaughtered the thundering herds of buffalo for their hides, ate the hump meat, and sometimes the tongue. Plains Indians who depended on the buffalo for a food supply ate the whole animal, after the women had skinned and butchered it.

The demise of the buffalo herds crushed the Indians as well.

Governor W. Lee O'Daniel once invited his supporters to a buffalo barbecue in Austin, probably a fund-raising event. A city-type flour salesman from Fort Worth, O'Daniel was invited to harvest a buffalo from a ranch near Rocksprings. It became a media event, attended by Texas Rangers and other notables. A buffalo bull was killed, and records show the governor did it, although insiders claim a Texas Ranger did some backup shooting.

An endangered species 50 years ago, the bison is making a comeback. *Farm and Ranch Living* magazine reports that the world's largest herd, 4,000 head, roams the 53,000-acre ranch of Roy Houck in South Dakota. The ranch switched from cattle to buffalo, which are slaughtered and the meat sold readily to gourmet food stores, health food stores, and supermarkets around the country.

There's a brisk market, too, for buffalo hides, mostly for decoration, according to the magazine.

Several herds of buffalo are found in Texas and others all over the plains ranch country.

"Despite being cantakerous (at roundup time), buffalo are hardy creatures and offer some advantages over cattle," said the report by Diane Sweet on the Houck operation. "They live longer and produce more calves . . . Buffalo steak and burgers are fine sources of protein. The flavor is difficult to distinguish from fine beef."

For many years, experiments have been conducted in crossing buffalo with beef cattle, producing an offspring usually called a "cattalo." While a few ranchers like the late Charles Goodnight of the Texas Panhandle were great boosters for the cross-breed, it never really caught on.

For the benefit of Strauss and others, buffalo cooking recipes are available. *American Heritage* magazine offered three samples of a "delicacy for dieters." Buffalo steak with wild rice dressing sounds delicious. So do buffalo prime ribs in a roasted salt jacket, and charbroiled buffalo steak.

Using these might help the former ambassador spread good will.

FAT FLEAS FOR SALE

To persons reared with country dogs, the term "flea market" is hardly attractive.

When first I saw a "flea market" sign, what passed my mind was who in the world would want to buy fleas — or even swap fleas?

Now that flea markets are flourishing, often where country

slickers sell junk and an occasional antique to city folks, flea marketing has become a growth industry.

This intelligence came from Clyde E. Johnson of Corsicana, who cashed in on the trend by peddling a statewide flea market directory.

The flea market, according to Oxford English Dictionary and a book called *In Europe* by G. S. Dougherty stems from a French term *marche aux puces* — market with fleas.

It described a place where so many second-hand articles were sold ''they are believed to gather fleas.''

What with flea collars and insecticides, one should find fleas scarce in a modern flea market, but from the looks of some markets and customers, the possibility still exists.

Directory publisher Johnson terms flea marketing a ''giant'' both for sellers and buyers, with Texas attracting dealers from throughout the nation.

Johnson urged people to ''beware of false flea markets'' which are nothing more than retail business establishments.

Thought has been given in our household to establishing a temporary stall in some flea market, or either hold a yard sale. We cannot have a garage sale because our garage is too full of stuff that needs to be sold.

We are greatly overstocked on bottles, some stored so long they must be approaching antique status, such as genuine ship's decanters that once held bourbon. We have enough to outfit the original Texas Navy.

After living more than 30 years in the same house (with the same wife) our closets are bursting and storerooms overflowing. Our daughter recently picked up — by request — a nice serving tray that was a wedding present years ago.

There are old tennis rackets . . . golf clubs . . . broken yard tools . . . baskets . . . one person in our household is a sucker for buying baskets, especially when we are on vacation.

If ever we took an inventory, doubtless rare goods would be discovered. I have suggested without success that we should carry everything into the yard and bring what is really needed back into the house. Enough would remain to stock a modest flea market.

The real prize, however, is a stockpile of ancient barbed wire which came with an old stock farm. Miles and miles of old barbed wire picked up in the pastures now is deposited in a barn, awaiting the opportunity to strike it rich.

A Dallas friend reported that old barbed wire brings high prices in a city flea market, and I have offered him a partnership to handle the sale. So far there has been no deal.

Meanwhile, Neiman-Marcus has profited from selling barbed wire, gilded, as swizzle sticks. It gives a little bit of Texas to the jet set.

And proves that some folks really know how to merchandise.

HOW FUR TO MONEY

That raccoon stealing from your garbage can may have a hide worth $20.

The fur business sometimes booms in Texas, according to Bill Brownlee of the Texas Parks and Wildlife Department. The pelts go mostly to western Europe and Japan for fur coats and fur trimming, and the high prices are pushing trapping activity to a near record level.

The number of licensed trappers in Texas jumped 10-fold during the late 1970s. Pelts can be sold in December and January, except muskrats and mink where the seasons run from Nov. 15 to Jan. 15.

Old-timers recall when coonskin coats for collegians and others caused many a rural resident to trap for profit in the winter. Starting in the 1930s, fur prices dropped to almost nothing, and raccoons and some other wild animals increased their mischief among crops and flocks without much interference from local folks.

Coons are the bread-and-butter item of fur trappers. In 1977 430,000 pelts were sold during the season at prices ranging from $1 to about $24, and now bring $10 to $15. There's no law against killing raccoons or other varmints at any time, but the pelts can be sold only during the two winter months.

Opossum hides are less valuable but nearly 200,000 were bought from Texas trappers. Ringtails, often taken by coon trappers and hunters, number 86,564 in the market place.

Bobcats produced high-priced fur, bringing up to $75 per pelt, but less now because of federal regulations on interstate shipments. Although the bobcat is near being an endangered species in parts of the United States, the spotted animal is flourishing in Texas where 15,900 bobcat pelts were sold in 1977.

Coyotes are big business, too. Nearly 50,000 hides were sold at $15 to $320 each. While the raccoon is the most common furbearing wild animal in Texas, coyotes are the most widespread, living all over the state. Because of depredations on livestock and game, bounties up to $100 per coyote are offered in more than a score of counties.

These hides are rendered non-salable because the bounty payer usually removes an ear or tail to prevent another bounty claim on the same dead coyote.

Brownlee believes man fights a hopeless war against the coyote. Though many are killed, the crafty doglike animal thrives in inhabited as well as isolated areas. It reproduces prolifically.

The game department's fur expert believes inhabited areas — contrary to the concerns of many environmentalists — can be overrun with wildlife, including unwanted varieties of birds, in a short time except for preventive measures and natural die off. As it is, the greatest toll among most wild varieties comes from natural die off, caused by starvation or disease in overpopulated areas.

Brownlee views the harvest by trappers as a benefit to the fur-bearing population as well as to mankind, a valuable and renewable resource which otherwise would be lost by death from natural causes.

Trapping for pelts is a seasonal occupation, and Brownlee estimates about 3,000 Texans are near-professionals. Most others are rural residents, often boys, seeking to earn a few extra dollars while getting rid of some predators.

Texas has a wide variety of furbearing animals. Nutria from marshlands along the coast are the only type trapped and sold around the year, Brownlee said. Texas has an increasing number of mountain lions, mostly traveling West Texas from the protection of Big Bend National Park.

More than 52,000 pelts from the unsociable striped skunks were sold in 1977, along with 3,236 from the civet cat (spotted skunk). Sales from gray foxes outnumbered red foxes 33,000 to 7,000. East Texans sold 4,063 mink hides while the lowest sale was 87 otter pelts, a species which may be put on the endangered list.

There's big money in trapping!

ACRES BY AIR MAIL

My father wrote an annual letter while we were attending the University of Texas back in the "dust bowl" days of the 1930s

"Dear Son," he said one April. "I am sending our last 40 acres by air mail . . . ''

This proved dad hadn't lost his sense of humor, even though he had lost nearly all his possessions and much of his health through a bank failure in Plainview, plus a drouth and windstorms which blew much of the Panhandle plains' topsoil across the broad expanse of Texas.

Two things recently serve to remind of those bleak days. One is the drouth which grips the state, plus an unusually windy spring that has brought duststorms repeatedly to Central Texas. Austin's official rainfall since last October (1970) totaled less than one inch.

The other reminder came from Walter E. Long, one of Austin's great citizens, who retired after years as manager of the chamber of commerce. It dealt with measurements made May 3, 1935, by the late Dr. E. P. Schoch, then a noted chemical engineer at the state university.

Dr. Schoch's data indicated one duststorm "rained down" 13 tons of solids per square mile over Travis County in a single day. This figured out to total 13,052 tons — more than 26 million pounds — of good earth blown from West Texas to settle in this county 400 miles away. So the reference to "air-mailing" the last 40 acres of a Hale County farm wasn't so far-fetched.

In succeeding years, the flat plains became an agricultural

LOEHLIN 81

garden spot of the world, thanks to irrigation from a vast underground reservoir, which is itself a diminishing resource. Many citizens are seeking new means to water the fertile plains, to reduce the blowing soil, and use it to grow food and fiber.

Such vast projects as bringing surplus water from the Mississippi or from the Pacific Northwest are suggested, all expensive and fraught with problems. Yet none seems more unattainable or expensive than putting men on the moon.

Texas drouths have come in 20-year cycles during our lifetime, and we hope the cycle is broken.

Duststorms seem to give energy to sustain people who live among them.

It also gave the plains people a special brand of humor, such as:

—A 4-year-old child fainted from the first raindrop in its life. Took a bucket of sand to revive the little tyke.

—It is too windy to plow when (1) a man can't hold a wet cowhide over the keyhole inside the house or (2) a log chain attached to the roof's eaves stands straight out from the breeze.

—Prairie dogs lost in the storm have gone down chimneys, thinking it was their hole.

—One man bet it ''never would rain again'' and was paid off. Let us hope the loser gets his money back.

A West Texas preacher once chided his congregation at a special meeting to pray for rain.

''Oh ye of little faith,'' he intoned. ''Where are your umbrellas?''

II

All You Want To Know About Overalls And More

SUSPENDERS ARE BACK IN STYLE

The news that men's suspenders are back in style comes as no surprise to some of us.

I never went out of style. For years I have worn suspenders on special occasions, and intend to keep right on doing so. My reason for wearing suspenders is simple: To hold up my pants.

Most of my suspenders' attire has nothing to do with any passing fashion. My elastic "braces" are used for hunting trips and outdoor work, where my pockets are likely to be weighted down with wrenches, knives, cartridges, pliers etc. There is nothing more refreshing or embarrassing than to have your trousers fall down on a winter morning when you are walking across a pasture with a rifle in one hand and a stool in the other, leaving nothing to support your pants. Suspenders can prevent this.

Fashion Dallas, a newspaper feature, recently termed suspenders the "look of the week."

The model was a clean-cut young man who looked like he might be so conservative (or pessimistic) that he wore both suspenders and a belt. I liked his suspenders, heavy brown and black striped and with loops attached to buttons on his trousers, fore and aft.

The model also wore a necktie which makes one suspect this is a Johnny-come-lately to the suspenders set. The only time I ever wear a necktie and suspenders together are to very infrequent "black tie" affairs, which the late Vice President Alben W. Barkley termed "putting on the heavy harness."

My formal suspenders once were white. These antiques are

now so relaxed they are really just shoulder straps.

In the working world where overalls are worn on manual jobs, such as carpentry, the straps and the pants are all together. These outfits are comfortable, with ample pockets and room to sit down or squat without injuring the wearer.

During hard times, you heard of "1-gallus farmers" who hadn't made enough crops to buy new overalls in three years. An exception is the old boy who has made a fortune and can wear whatever he prefers.

In recent years, fashion chic has encouraged young women to wear jeans or overalls such as nobody would have worn in earlier years if they could avoid it.

I am concerned that the new "western" fashions will hurt my image by putting so many pavement cowhands into clothes like I've worn for years.

Take cowboy boots. When I started wearing boots several years ago, my footwear often was regarded as an affectation. Actually, it was for foot comfort and to keep from stepping on thorns and rattlesnakes.

Now the fashion magazines are full of cowboy boot advertisements, with undernourished models looking very unwestern. Many city folks yearn for rural clothing if not for country living.

My generation tried to escape the "country" image. As a high school youth, I once purchased a pair of "spats," a little overcoat for the ankles worn over low-quarter shoes. Only real dudes and Britishers wore spats. Mine were gray. They drew few compliments but frequent headshakes from my elders.

Good may come from the current trend toward basics in men's clothing.

Suspender buttons must reappear on men's trousers. The clip-on type just don't get the job done for a man in my shape, which is tapered from the middle.

With old-time suspenders and comfortable pants, a man can sit down without splitting his wallet pocket, or something worse.

THE ELITE WEAR OVERALLS

A young friend of ours employed in the headquarters of an oil and cattle magnate in a Dallas skyscraper confided that staff members were considering a change of office uniforms from western wear to "bib jeans."

"You mean overalls?" we asked, incredulous.

"I guess you'd call them overalls," was the reply.

While our knowledge of "bib jeans" isn't up to date, you are reading an expert on "overalls." Only it was pronounced "overhauls" by most associates of rural yesteryears before we became a "white collar worker" in a colored shirt.

Recently, overalls are the "in" garment for urban youth displaying disregard for the Establishment in its fancy clothes.

This reverses the historic trend of overall-wearing. Originally, only men wore overalls except when some Daisy Mae character of the backwoods had nothing except Pa's hand-me-down clothing. Once a follower of the American Dream had it made, he shed his overalls in favor of a linen suit and a starched collar.

We did research on the overall situation here a couple of years ago, before the latest bib jean-overall kick. We concluded that real overalls are hard to find. Department store clerks would show you "jump suits" and other uniforms with little alligators embroidered on the pocket. These are fit for nothing rougher than mowing the lawn, or driving to the store for refreshments after such labor.

Such gear does not deserve to be mentioned in the same class as real blue-and-white striped overalls.

We found an old-time carpenter wearing genuine overalls, with an apron attached. He advised confidentially that a J. C. Penney store in the suburbs kept authentic overalls in stock, but we never could find the store.

For the benefit of the multitude who apparently can't distinguish overalls from a jump suit, let us explain that real overalls are both sturdy and naturally air-conditioned. They are made of durable denim and held up by heavy suspenders of the same material, buttoned to the bib with metal fasteners.

A smart overall buyer gets them plenty loose, for the air

funneling up the pants legs and down from the topside provides readymade evaporative cooling for the wearer.

For an outdoor workman, overalls offer certain hazards. The suspenders catch on brambles, and all kinds of loose chaff and shavings drop inside the garment, fore and aft, even if the wearer is careful. Fortunately, most such trash drops right on through if your overalls are large enough.

Part of our early experience was in "coveralls," which also were called "union-alls" or "union-hauls" possibly denoting manufacture by the United Textile Workers.

Coveralls are all right in cool weather, but for a hot Texas summer day, nothing beats overalls.

Perhaps the new fashion in bib-jeans and-or overalls is nature's way of preparing people for the Energy Crunch. When air conditioning goes off, overalls are the best working clothes, if you have to wear something.

In a doctoral dissertation that may be more informative than most, a University of Texas Ph.D wrote that the neck is a thermostat for the human body, largely controlling the owner's personal comfort.

This scientific disclosure confirms our long-held theory about clothing. And it also explains why we consider neckties to be torture devices, perhaps the inspiration for the hangman's noose. Neckties upset one's personal ecology, particularly in hot weather.

Not so with overalls. Full-cut from Texas cotton (not sleazy synthetic stuff), overalls were invented for wearing where the wind blows free. We don't know how bib jeans will fit into Dallas office decor, but it should give the wearers some sense of independence, even in air-conditioned splendor.

"DENIMS ARE DYNAMITE"

A fashion writer said "denims are dynamite" again.

The whole range of attire for both sexes, from rough work clothes to "formal" wear, is being manufactured from the fabric that Columbus reportedly used for sails to discover the New World.

Denim USA, a trade organization, reports that denim jeans sell for the equivalent of $75 in Soviet Russia, when they are available. When a group of Russian athletes once came to Austin, the whole team went home wearing blue jeans bought at local stores.

The denim boom, which is international, is a boon to cotton farmers, since 90 per cent of denim clothing is pure cotton. There are denim tuxedos, evening dresses, hats, shoes, and even a denim lining for a mink coat and a denim-covered Bible.

Although the cloth is among the oldest known, its popularity for wearing apparel started during the California gold rush in 1849-50 when Levi Strauss started manufacturing pants for miners from the material he took West. It has been a latter-day gold rush for Levi Strauss Co., which now has more than 50 factories around the world, and there are other manufacturers.

The denims-for-everybody movement really started in World War II when people looked for durable and practical clothing. Many women went to work in factories and donned the once masculine apparel. Denim also attracted converts in the U.S. Navy where it was standard gear.

The early '60s saw the boom skyrocket around the world, partly the result of the export of western movies by the U.S., where blue jeans were as much a part of the hero as his big hat and 6-gun.

Denim USA claims that despite the fabric's worldwide popularity ''for some reason, no other country has been able to produce denim to the consumer's satisfaction.''

The civil rights marches and ''return to nature'' movement among U.S. youth in the 1950s and 1960s also added to denim's popularity, for most of the demonstrators and city-reared outdoorspeople wore denims. After that came ''stylish'' denim clothing in suits and dresses, often costing in the $100-$200 range.

This is a far cry from the $3.95 blue jeans and $4.95 overalls of our boyhood: which neither sex wore for ''dress-up.''

Indigo, the blue color used in most denim clothing, is called the oldest natural dye in the world. It was found in the fabrics buried with the Egyptian pharaohs in the Pyramids.

A German chemist synthesized indigo nearly 100 years ago, and this became the well-known coloring for most denims in the U.S. But the company making the dye seriously considered dropping it in 1966, just before the blue-jean craze took hold.

One development the inventors never expected is the faded-denim fad. Young Americans go to great effort to fade their trousers and make them look as scruffy as possible, cutting off the legs to leave ragged edges a la Daisy Mae of hillbilly comic fame.

Some laundries charge high prices for giving a garment a quick worn and faded appearance.

One family we know almost broke up over denim blue jeans. The teen-age son came home on vacation wearing a beat up, faded pair of jeans that he had gone to much trouble and expense giving the wornout look.

The youth's mother found the dirty jeans among his clothing, and gave them to the yard man.

She never was able to explain to her offspring that she wasn't just trying to help him, and she never understood why her son wanted to go around looking like a refugee from the cotton patch.

A PIECE OF STRING

A piece of string brightened the lives of several people around our neighborhood.

It started in a very ordinary way.

The man of the house (me) was out front cutting some brush into short lengths and tying it into bundles so the garbage truck would pick it up.

Along came a sweet-faced lady who stopped to ask where I bought the ball of string I was using.

"— at a hardware store," I replied.

She sighed: "I've walked to two grocery stores this morning trying to buy some string and neither one has any."

"How much do you need?" I asked.

She held her hands apart about two feet.

"Just enough to make a new cord for my window shade."

"Well, help yourself," I offered, rolling off a couple of yards of the string, then cutting it with a knife.

She thanked me kindly, and walked on down the street.

I reported the incident to my wife, along with the other pedestrian traffic passing my brush-cutting operation. I dismissed it as just a lady who was willing to ask a strange man for a piece of string.

Certainly, it was no big deal, even if I had given her the whole ball, for I keep other string around the house.

A few hours later, the doorbell rang. My wife answered. I overheard their conversation.

The visitor asked if the man who gave her the string lived in the house.

"Yes."

"Well, I want him to have these cookies," she said, handing over a decorated tin filled with chocolate chip macaroons.

"You sweet person. You didn't need to do this."

The lady said she wanted to. The conversation revealed that her name was Wallis, and she lived a few blocks away. Although we had lived in the same area for years, we'd never had occasion to make acquaintance, until a piece of string opened the way.

Everyone who heard this story smiled and commented happily about it.

This isn't told for any approval of my "generosity". If I hadn't been blocking the sidewalk, it probably would never have happened.

But it does reflect how insignificant kindness may produce unexpected returns. Often, I have criticized myself for failing to pay heed to the needs of others or to help when it should have been given.

Our new friend proved appreciation is still alive and well, and her response was a reward that extended far beyond our household. The cookies, incidentally, were delicious.

City folks often tend to overlook the value of being neighborly. In rural areas, it has long been the custom to return a favor just as soon as possible. If the neighbors down the road bring you a fresh pie, they go home with a sack of fresh garden vegetables. Not that any barter was expected. It is just the way to do things, where everybody benefits.

Many years ago, Guy de Maupassant wrote a famous short story titled *A Piece of String*.

It is about a frugal farmer in rural France who picked up a piece of string from the street while he was in the village. The harness-maker, who didn't like the farmer, saw him do it, but couldn't tell what was picked up.

Shortly, the town cryer announced a traveler had lost his purse on the street. The harness-maker told the mayor he saw the farmer pick it up. The farmer was hailed into the mayor's office and accused of stealing the purse, which of course he denied.

An illiterate villager had found the purse and soon returned it to the owner. But no amount of explaining convinced the villagers that the farmer hadn't gotten the illiterate one to return the purse. In a few months, the farmer died with a heart broken over man's inhumanity to man.

Our piece of string may never be as famous. But it certainly produced a happier ending.

LOOKING AT YOUR OWN GALL BLADDER

"There it is . . . your gall bladder!" the pleased young man announced.

I was an interested observer, since medical science had been looking for the thing for four days.

"It's the wispy little white thing right here by your liver," he continued.

Glad to meet my liver, too, I thought.

The picture on the screen kept changing as the operator kept moving the viewer back and forth, up and down, across my well-oiled belly.

It didn't hurt.

I lay there on the slab watching with fascination as my insides were screened like a good science show.

The gentle, bearded young man kept up an interesting patter about his profession and his patients, all the while moving the pointer around my right lower rib cage.

"Wow! There it is — the gallstone." He stopped the moving and seemed as excited as if he'd just discovered a whale.

"Hey, how about that?" I remarked. "Where is it?"

"The gall bladder is the wispy white, and the stone is the small round black spot," he said.

"Why that's *my* gallstone," I almost shouted, as if realizing for the first time I was watching my own show. Until then, it was like two grown people on an electronic Easter egg hunt.

Now that we had found it, the young man — not being a physician — declined all comment on what would be done with this great discovery.

But this, my first experience with sonography, was worth the trip to the hospital.

Radiologists had spent the two previous days searching without success for my gall bladder with conventional equipment. Nothing showed on the x-rays. It was a depressing and nauseating experience started a week earlier with a monumental bellyache.

Then my doctor ordered the sonograph. No pills. No pain. No discomfort. The target was located in less than 10 seconds as if it is all in a day's work.

Physicians call it the "ping" test because it pings to outline the object. It is a development in the field of physics.

"About half of my patients are pregnant women," said the sonography technician. You should hear the parents scream when they see the baby for the first time on the screen."

One mother at another hospital, I learned, received a sonography of her unborn babe and showed it to her visitors during the nine days before the child was born.

"You should have made it into a Christmas card," I suggested.

Actually, sonography — the use of sound waves — came into first full development in World War II, largely the work of University of Texas scientists. They developed it to help the Navy detect enemy submarines.

Geophysicists for years have used the echoed sound tech-

nique to study underground formations while looking for oil
and gas.

Sonography has been actively used in medicine for about
10 years. You will be hearing much more about it in the future.

DON'T PITY THE MILKMAN

With very little regret, we read that the milk deliveryman is
passing from the American scene.

Back in the 1930s Depression-Dust Bowl days, your correspondent was a teen-ager delivering milk twice daily in the
South Plains community of Plainview.

After this experience, any occupation including newspaper-
ing is comparatively soft.

Before making twice-daily deliveries to homes — mostly
over unpaved streets — at 15¢ a quart for milk, 40¢ a gallon, it
was necessary to extract same from more than one hundred
Jersey cows. This also was a twice-daily performance, starting at
1:30 a.m. (middle of the night, seven days a week).

After straining, cooling, and bottling the milk, we delivered it.

Neither snow, nor rain, nor sandstorm stopped the
milkman on his appointed round.

Biting dogs were a constant menace. So were loose roller
skates. Some dog owners during the Depression years seemed to
consider the deliveryman's leg a good diet for their pets.

We knew the disposition of every dog in town, and to this
day have a deep dislike for Spitz dogs and a lasting distrust of
some other breeds, such as the German Shepherd.

Today, school officials say many children don't know that
milk comes from cows. They believe it comes from cartons and
cans.

Rather than just showing students the pictures of an automated dairy on the school projector, it would be interesting to
take them on a 1-day trip with the milkman, from cow to customer. It would be educational, along lines the sociologists now
call ''work experience.'' We just used the short form — work.

For such a trip, the children would need to be up and

breakfasted long before dawn (an imposition on many parents, no doubt).

The youngsters would meet many more nice people (and dogs) than the other kind. They would get plenty of exercise and some outside air, unfortunately less fresh than during the unpolluted yesteryear. Sleeping should pose no problem at the end of such a day.

The daily deliveryman (or boy) is disappearing along with the elevator operator and Pullman porter. Higher-paying jobs with better hours and working conditions are available than those formerly held by the deliveryman. Distributors struggle to control labor costs.

But you can't beat the old system for character building. And if milk sells for a dollar a pint, it is a bargain in my estimation, considering the effort put forth by cow and human to get the stuff delivered.

These days, we just turn off the alarm and go back to sleep when we dream of the good old days in the milk business.

SLEEP THAT KNITS THE RAVELED SLEEVE OF CARE . . .

It was nearly midnight on the last weary night of the Legislature's session, and a small boy slept soundly on the carpeted floor in one corner of the House of Representatives.

Occasional sounds of the public address system and people scurrying about the brightly-lit chamber didn't bother the exhausted lad one bit.

Which caused a group of tired adults, waiting for the Insurance Conference Committee to report, to discuss sleeping under extraordinary circumstances.

Fred Agnich, a Republican representative from Dallas who helped discover oil in the jungles of Sumatra, recalled the night he stumbled into a swamp and slept until daybreak with a fallen tree limb for a pillow and his legs under water.

Bill Braecklein, Democrat, Dallas lawyer, added: "In the Army, I got so tired on long marches that I literally was asleep on my feet and still walking."

A newsman spoke of having slumbered soundly in an empty wagon bouncing over rutted roads as a pair of mules noisily pulled him home. That couldn't happen in a motor vehicle, by the way, because a horse or mule knows where he's going whether or not the driver does.

Continuing the subject next day, photographer Ted Powers of the Associated Press told a grisly sleeping tale.

After lengthy combat on Iwo Jima in World War II, Marine rifleman Powers sought rest and protection just below a friendly machine gun emplacement, overlooking a trail used by the enemy.

Next morning when Powers awoke, 19 dead Japanese soldiers lay scattered along the trail, the nearest almost within reach of the battle-weary Powers. The whole skirmish had been fought right over Powers' sleeping form without waking him.

. . . As one who can sleep through a hailstorm under a tin roof, we feel quite sorry for persons bothered by insomnia. Sleep is a true blessing as well as refreshing.

. . . One of our favorite deep-sleep stories was told by our mother-in-law, the late Mrs. R. R. English of Haskell and Plainview.

As a young lady in the West Texas ranch country, she attended an occasional big party at some ranch headquarters. Guests rode for miles in buggies and wagons or horseback. Very small children and babies were bedded down in the buggy or wagon in the outside darkness after growing tired of the festivities inside.

When the partied-out parents finally hitched up and drove home toward dawn, often miles away, they were sometimes horrified to discover that pranksters at the party had switched the sleeping children around and nearly everybody got home with the wrong offspring.

It usually took a day or so to return the youngsters to the right homes.

And it says something about the prank-playing younger generation in "the good old days."

ENOUGH TO MAKE A WELL MAN ILL

After watching the real life drama of a hospital, watching soap operas and other daytime television seemed dull.

The only thing worse than being homebound in the summer, observed a sympathetic friend, is watching the picture tube during daylight hours. Recently we had the opportunity — if that's the word — to review TV during the hours when ordinary people are off working somewhere. There was nothing else to do. I had to stay in the house because of my eye problem.

Strangely, the eye specialist said watching television is all right in my case since all I had to do was stare straight ahead. Reading requires eye movement, which is harmful to a newly repaired retina.

Thus I became a sort of handcuffed TV observer and headline scanner.

Starting with the best: Weekday morning news programs are all right, generally better in my opinion than the evening shows. The evening experts spent most of the time giving dramatic readings of ordinary news copy, while the morning types at least have something original to offer occasionally.

At the risk of alienating friends and family, I must confess the midday soap operas turned me off completely. I tried. Lord knows I tried to break the boredom by hearing the tangled woes of the soapers. But I simply never finished a whole program. Maybe they never end. I didn't wait to see.

Maybe a person just out of the hospital really isn't that interested in the fictitious problems on TV. The midday soap operas gag me.

I did manage to watch replays of black and white movies. Remember Judy Garland and Mickey Rooney the teen-agers? The cooking programs were more interesting, as was the series on how to grow old gracefully.

Religious television, I learned, is BIG. One whole network is devoted to such programs, and some are rather good. At least the shows are wholesome, even if the religion may be commercialized.

For whatever it means to a country where church-going has declined sharply, a television station manager says the demand for time for religious programs far exceeds the amount available.

And these get through to where most of the people are — at home.

My conclusion is that daytime television is 90 per cent boring. My day's high point was nap time. This can become habit-forming. The Houston Medical Center is a lot more interesting than what I saw on the tube.

After hours of preparation, in 15 minutes a noted eye surgeon, Dr. Alice McPherson, fused my torn retina back into place by cryogenics, a process involving very low temperature gas. Don't ask me for the details.

Texas, especially Houston, is world-renowned for medical care. The eye treatment center is just a small part of a vast complex that brings ailing people from all over the world.

Arabian princes, Latin Americans, Europeans . . . they come from everywhere. The next bed was occupied by a young Mexican physics graduate with a much more serious problem than mine. His father, a nuclear medicine physician from Mexico City, brought him to Houston.

The driver to the airport related that he'd help carry 24 persons from Amsterdam to catch a plane for home — after being treated at the medical center. They came as a group, accompanied by a physician.

Little wonder these made soap dramas seem pretty unreal.

TELEPHONE IN THE BATHROOM

The height of luxury, I have always thought, would be to have a telephone in your bathroom.

This pinnacle has never been achieved around our house, although half the calls, when I am at home alone, come when your correspondent is in the bathroom, usually naked and often wet.

A telephone is just across the hall from our bathroom, which is upstairs.

Time after time, when the phone rang so insistently I knew it was important if not actually an emergency, I have leaped wringing wet from my bath shower, grabbed a towel and skidded to the phone.

Often, the phone stops ringing just as I lift the receiver, leaving me worried about what vital information I had missed.

Just as frequently, someone wishes to chat with my wife. Since I am handy, the message(s) are relayed through me that a certain store was holding a shoe sale or ''weren't the electric bills frightful this month?''

By the time this discourse is over, I am nearly dry and shivering. Maybe I'm old-fashioned but I have never had the courage to tell a woman I am wet and naked and couldn't she call back later.

I am convinced that Ma Bell has somehow connected our telephone to the plumbing, because so many calls come while I am, as the old school gentlemen would say, "taking my ablutions."

Once in a while if a norther is blowing, the doorbell rings also. So I grab the towel, wrap it around my middle and set a record for the 20-yard dash to the front door, rather than let the postman leave notice that a package has been returned to the North Austin post office. It is a 5-mile roundtrip and a 20-minute wait in line at the post office next day (if I fail to catch the postman on the second ring). The important package usually turns out to be tulip bulbs or a record album which we hadn't ordered.

A few times we have enjoyed the luxury of a telephone in the bathroom at expensive hotels in the days when I traveled on an expense account. The problem here was that I seldom knew anybody in these distant places. I could spend a whole day in the bathroom and never use the phone unless I called the hotel clerk to find out how much this was costing the company.

Cynics have advised me that a bathroom telephone can be dangerous, that it carries electricity which can be very harmful to one's health when the customer's feet are in the water or the body is otherwise grounded.

I don't know about this, but am willing to risk it. In fact I once did survive the experience. On doctor's orders, I sat in a tub of hot water for 30 minutes four times a day. Since I was the only person at home during most of these set-tos, I received numerous telephone calls, including wrong numbers and child voices wanting to know if Mike could come over to play.

For fear of breaking a leg slipping on the bathroom tile, I had the phone company install a cord long enough for the upstairs phone to be carried into the bathroom. Happily, I was never electrocuted but I did feel a little silly sitting in a tub of water discussing the next garden club meeting with some woman I barely knew.

The caller usually commenced by asking if she was ''interrupting lunch'' or anything. I never could bring myself to reply, ''Oh, no! I was just sitting here in the bathtub waiting for your call.''

When we first moved into our house, the telephone number was just one digit different from the city's only obstetrician. Austin has many obstetricians today, but during World War II just one practiced here. Apparently most mothers deliver babies at night. We regularly got wrong number calls between midnight and dawn, from anguished fathers reporting ''doctor, we think the baby's coming. What do we do?''

Tempting as it was to offer free medical advice, we gave the caller the doctor's home number, which we kept beside the phone. Then I would often lie awake for hours wondering whose baby, what kind, and did they make it to the hospital in time.

Our first neighbors here were a splendid older couple, who were newlyweds in Oklahoma when it was Indian Territory. At his 90th birthday party, he recalled being nine years old when the telephone was invented. He was grown before anybody convinced him the message wasn't just somebody shouting through a hollow wire.

Now telephones are everywhere. The other day, while I was alone in an elevator at the University of Texas Barker History Center, the phone in the elevator rang. I was afraid to pick up the receiver for fear somebody would tell me the elevator was stuck between floors. By the time I had regained composure and been deposited on the ground floor, I wished I'd had the gumption to pick up the phone and reply ''Governor's Office'' or something else clever.

It seems incredible today that life existed without Alexander Graham Bell's invention. For three dollars you can call your kinfolks in California and talk 10 minutes, which is a much better bargain than 20 cents for a stamp that may take a week to deliver the mail.

Still, one reason men and women head for the hills to relax is it takes them away from the telephone and maybe even away from taking baths every day while wondering who's ringing the phone.

NIX TO MEDICAL REPORTS

They are going too far in requiring every presidential candidate to make public his medical record.

It is all right to require financial disclosure.

But asking a person to publicize his physical ailments is too much. Even my physician won't show me my medical report, perhaps for fear of frightening the patient. We just discuss it across his desk in a professional manner.

The great electrical engineer, Charles Steinmetz, once commented wisely that the world's work gets done mostly by people who do not feel well. We agree. While some workers take off at the slightest sniffle, a physical malaise seems to drive others to greater effort.

This is a bit beside the point, but an Indian journalist from Delhi who visited here said most Americans eat too much to think clearly. Hunger, such as abounds in India, sharpens the senses, he said. I don't know about this, having spent a lifetime trying to avoid hunger.

The medical reports on all candidates for president of the United States indicate they are virtually a squad of mature athletes, as former President Ford really is. George Wallace is an exception, but even the Alabama governor missed just one day from campaigning after an aide dropped him. How many other adults could do as well after being dropped?

The hardest part physically of public office is the campaign to get elected. Candidates fly around the country at a hectic pace, in good weather and bad, often eating food of indifferent quality, and being required to put on a happy face for strangers when they'd much rather be at home in bed. It is a grueling process, and one wishes there could be a better way to select the leaders of our government.

Franklin D. Roosevelt, the man who held the presidency longest, more than 12 years, was the poorest physical specimen to hold the office in our lifetime, unless it was Lyndon B. Johnson, who suffered a massive heart attack before assuming the office. Roosevelt was badly crippled by poliomyelitis before being elected in 1932.

Roosevelt's physical condition was so bad that he never should have run for a fourth term in 1944. But the nation was engaged in a deadly war and didn't want to change leaders. Vice-President Harry Truman became chief executive at Roosevelt's death in 1945 and proved to be a surprisingly good president. Often, the challenge makes a man or woman — and perfect health isn't any requirement for success.

Some of the greatest people whom we have known have never been good physical specimens, although they usually try to protect the health they have.

Knowing one's own limitations is often more important than having a first-class physique.

If this sounds like sour grapes from one who still has four years of eligibility left in high school football — never having been invited to try out for the team — perhaps it is. Physically, we are qualified to be president. Our ailments are about equal to those of the men who are running, even Lloyd Bentsen's occasional eye twitch.

We have both eyes and both kidneys, which is more than some candidates have. But the left eye can't be corrected to 20-20.

THE CONFUSING NUMBERS GAME

The pleasant-voiced lady asked on the phone if I would like to have one of those cash-savings accounts where I could do my banking with a plastic card inserted in an electronic terminal.

"How can you keep dishonest people from drawing money from my account?" we inquired.

''Every customer has his own secret number.''

''Where do you keep the secret number?''

''In your head,'' she replied.

''My gosh, lady, I already have so many numbers I can't remember any of them.''

''This one is easy.''

''What if I give the machine the wrong number?''

''It will keep your card and you have to go to the bank with identification to get it back.''

So, I decided I would just keep doing my banking business at the bank instead of sticking a plastic card into some device at the supermarket.

Just count me as confused over the numbers game.

Just as I am about to brand on my mind that my home zip code is 78705, word comes from Washington that the post office experts are considering 9-digit zip codes. Ye gods! Mine has been changed three times at the same address already, and I still have a supply of stationery showing me at Austin 22, Texas.

This is only the tip of my personal iceberg. I cannot remember the license number on either automobile, or my driver's license number, or my Social Security number, or my hospital insurance group number, or any bank account numbers, or my bank safety box number.

I envy people who can remember everybody's telephone number as well as the names of every person they have met in the last 20 years. I can remember those I met 20 years ago better than the ones I met last week, although I once forgot my college roommate's name.

Once I could remember half of the license number on one automobile, but we traded it off. The number was 254, which is easy to remember because that's how many counties there are in Texas.

But telephone numbers are something else. More than once, when working in an office with multi-line telephones. I caught myself dialing myself. I dialed the number I was talking from (which I could read on the phone), and the rotary system made the lights flash an incoming call. That was me, friends, thinking I had called home but only managing to find myself still at the office.

It is comforting to know that this gap of mentality (which I hear others also suffer) doesn't necessarily keep me from being reasonably normal in other ways. I know a very distinguished professor who has to write down a telephone number after he looks it up in the directory, because he can't remember it long enough to get the number dialed.

Computers for the home are on the way, and are claimed to solve many of the problems of faulty-memory persons. Instead of having to dial one or zero plus area code and seven digits, for example, I can punch a single number and the computer will ring my mother in West Texas.

I can hardly wait to see what other miracles can be wrought. Could I program the thing to make a bank deposit for me at the supermarket?

Since I haven't the faintest idea how the engineers can put all this information on a silicon chip, I am rather embarrassed that I can't keep it stored in a brain which has been barely used during my lifetime.

Ordinary people will not understand all this, but many of the younger generation talk about computers like they were discussing the price of groceries.

A sophomore engineering student at Texas A&M tried to explain to me the other day a new program in which he will be involved to test the thermodynamics of the space shuttle aircraft at the space center in Houston. A stunned expression must have occupied my face although I pretended to understand what he was talking about. The whole thing is already programmed into a computer.

This young fellow also had a pocket computer programmed (among other things) to take the day, month, and year of your birth and translate into current information.

I remember one thing the gadget predicted about me.

My health will be low the day after Christmas.

The new computer terminal arrived at my front door at 3 a.m. one morning, just as Managing Editor Terry Walsh said it would.

One of the wonders of this technical age is that nobody can predict what will happen next — such as having a large corporation deliver a computer terminal to your residence in the middle of the night. It's one of many things I never learned in journalism school.

The Dallas Morning News Austin Bureau leaped into the 20th century with the arrival of its new equipment. Everything will be faster, just when I had reached an age when a slowdown would be more appropriate.

Just as airlines planes now fly so fast you hardly have time to enjoy a drink or meal between stops, so the news industry is racing ahead with the speed of sound. We'll leave it to the customers to decide whether the product is improved.

I never have learned to trust automation completely, but if science can land men on the moon — and bring them back — there's reason to believe robots can put out a newspaper.

Actually, people are still the most important thing about this organization, increasingly important. News reporting is a peculiarly human operation, requiring judgment and good taste. Faster communication requires quicker and better judgment.

When I joined the state Capitol press corps some years ago as a teletypist-office boy, the teletype was about as newfangled as computers are today. The machines replaced the telegraph, whose operators were a breed of real characters. Some telegraphers adjusted to sending words over teletypes, but others just gave up.

Generations of men and machines have come and gone. Journalism schools now are called communications schools, and they give good mechanical training to students.

Still, nobody heard in class what to do with a computer terminal on his doorstep at 3 a.m. I went outdoors in my pajamas and carried the thing into the living room, until I could enlist my wife's help in loading it into our car for delivery to our news office. Why it was sent to me at such an ungodly hour is too complicated to explain here.

My first impulse after my wife claimed she never slept a wink after 3 a.m. when the gadget arrived was to hook it up and notify the Dallas office that Morehead hereafter would be operating a news bureau from his home. The terminals look like a portable typewriter which can transmit by telephone, except they contain a mini-computer which costs thousands of dollars.

It is easy to see we can get so automated it will be unnecessary to get out of bed in the morning. Just punch a button. A machine lights up. It does all the work, including breakfast in bed.

One old-time columnist before all this automation came out used to dream between drinks of inventing a column machine. To an outsider, or even an employer, columns such as this may seem easy to write. When they think we are loafing, actually we are pondering what wisdom can be imparted next to an expectant public.

My friend's column machine would have been programmed to crank out funny, happy, dramatic, tragic, analytical, profound, or other type essays just by punching a button according to the subject matter desired. It would have to be programmed with a good many essays to keep from repeating itself too frequently. The idea has merit.

Another writer friend once tried to sell an article to *Reader's Digest* about odd happenings when automatic equipment goes wrong. One example he used was the delivery of 22,000 copies of the same issue of *Time* magazine to a subscriber in Bozeman, Mont., when the addressing machinery fouled up.

The *Reader's Digest* man didn't think that was funny. What if it happened to them?

I decided several years ago that automatic communication offers limits, if not genuine perils. We were sending a story in ''takes'' — a page of copy at a time — from the Democratic National Convention in Chicago to *The News* office in Dallas on a midnight deadline.

Later we learned that one page never reached its destination. Weeks later, it was reported having been received at a cotton brokerage office in Tokyo. They wanted us to pay the bill.

THE BIG WINNER

From the looks of my mail, I should be rich.

Seldom does the postman ringeth but the mail brings a beautiful assortment of contest literature, with my name (usually R. Morehead) already neatly typed upon the grand prize line.

Assuming I already have plenty of money, the contest managers tempt me with offers of free condominiums on Cape Cod, a Mercedes Benz sedan with a station wagon as a spare vehicle, fishing tackle, television sets, field glasses, and even enticing ''mystery gifts'' for me to open just by getting my entry in early.

The trouble is, I spend 15 minutes and a 20-cent stamp mailing back my entry, and that's the last I ever hear of it.

Once an outfit in California, from which I ordered some fancy-sounding but rather worthless gadgets such as home repair kits for my lounging chair, did send me a ball-point pen. I lost it.

Years ago, I was luckier. Once I won a bicycle in a drawing at a Plainview store where my parents had bought me a fancy $18.75 suit. Probably the bicycle was worth more than the suit, but it really did me little good. We lived in the country. No pavement. No sidewalks. The tires promptly went flat from cactus thorn punctures, and the wheels developed odd twists from hitting obstacles in our pasture, such as frozen cow patties.

The same store did give freebies which I wish I had saved. The defeat of Germany in World War I and default on its currency made the German mark of 1920 worthless. Now, I hear, the kaiser's old money is worth about as much as U.S. currency.

I had millions of marks in my youth, which we used for play money. From the volume of contest mail, it appears we should be able to pay everybody's taxes with the winnings.

Four contest brochures which came in recent mail represent about half a million dollars in potential cash and assorted luxuries for yours truly.

Think what would happen if every American could win a mere $100,000, for example.

If I didn't misplace my decimal, this calculates to a total for all Americans of more than $2 trillion! We could pay the national debt, which is just past the first trillion dollar figure. Of course, the feds would have to tax away half our winnings, which it always does. We'd still have about $50,000 apiece, which would keep one alive through 1982 if the inflation rate doesn't rise.

Let the president and congress eliminate the middle man (the postal service) and run one big contest from Washington, using franked (postage free) mail for the purpose.

I haven't figured yet where the money would come from to pay people to deliver all this free mail, but we already get so much postage-exempt mail from our leaders in Washington that somebody up there must know how a postal service can operate with so much free business.

The national contest which I have in mind would be something like a lottery, except everyone would win.

There must be something wrong with my idea, but politicians have been elected on worse platforms.

Once, in California, from whence come so many bright ideas, a man named Townsend suggested giving everybody over 65 a check for $200 a month just to help the economy and keep them from want. This was offered seriously, but many regarded it as a crackpot suggestion at the time.

Later, Washington adopted different, more complicated plans for sharing the wealth, which have become so much a part of our economy that nobody apparently can slow the currency printing presses.

Like some of my other ideas, the Morehead Plan to make every American a lifetime-security contest winner may have technical flaws. But if you don't think about it, surely it has appeal.

LOVE THOSE GERANIUMS

Do philodendron feel?

Evidence gathered by a New York scientist that plants have emotions, much like humans and other animals, has shaken our household in recent days.

We hardly retain any sense of privacy, sitting among the pot plants, since reading of Cleve Backster's research awhile ago.

Our ivy seems to be inclining a leafy ear to catch our every word.

And the philodendron in our study looks almost defiant. We have pruned away yards of philodendron tentacles over the years to keep the plant from carrying off our typewriter. Now Backster comes with the new theory that life signals can be transmitted freely between plants and people, and our philodendron points its fingers at us.

When we confided this information to an old friend, Ted Powers, an Associated Press photographer, he responded with sympathy.

''You need a vacation,'' said Powers.

Obviously, our friend has been too busy taking pictures and being president of the Headliners Club and such cultural organizations as the Friday Old Fitz Club to keep abreast of scientific development.

By using electronic measurements similar to those of the polygraph (lie detector), the Backster Research Foundation has discovered that plants emote like people, and pets. A sensitive flower will react in sympathy when you break an egg into the skillet, for there goes life.

Plants even develop friendly feeling toward certain individuals (jealous gardeners call these the ''green thumbs''). The plants show hostility toward some other people.

Our experience with gardenia culture is an example of the latter. Our very presence seems to have stimulated a suicide syndrome. The beautiful blooms dropped from the plant on our way home from the nursery. Then the whole carcass curled up and died, despite our elaborate preparation to keep it happy and healthy.

The Backster theory calls to mind that the hardiest plants around our house came from the hardiest people we ever knew. Perhaps these do perpetuate the qualities of the givers, and certainly they have brought brightness, strength, and joy into our lives.

A durable croton was brought to us by a pioneer lady, who

has since died. She rode stagecoaches in West Texas as a girl, and lived to watch the jets fly.

Our night-blooming cereus has ancestry lost in antiquity. We inherited the plant from a longtime friend whose wife grew cereus for almost half a century.

Our philodendron was the gift of a young woman to our 10-year-old daughter, then confined with the measles. That was many years ago.

Like the youth it represents, our philodendron keeps "coming on." Sometimes it gets out of bounds, but we do sense purpose in its course and take comfort in its presence.

. . . Especially since the scientists say it can sympathize with humans.

MEMORIES OF "SWEET SUE"

Once upon a time, the organist for the First Baptist Church in Plainview played "Sweet Sue" as an offertory.

This recollection came to mind the Sunday a group of University of Texas students conducted the worship service at our church. They clapped hands, played guitars, and provided such unusual musical accompaniment as "Feeling Groovy," "Impossible Dream," and a rock number from a new Broadway show.

Some of the grayer heads were a bit shaken by the youth's departure from a church style that has been little changed since Martin Luther, but generally the performance drew approval from both young and old.

Having been young once ourselves, some time back, the memory of "Sweet Sue" at the Baptist church still brings a smile of satisfaction.

This happened at a Sunday evening service, when the unmistakeable strains of the popular song came through in dignified tone from the pipe organ played by Guy Wood, then director of music at Wayland.

A gifted musician, Wood was a favorite with the students. On that Sunday afternoon, he urged students to attend the Baptist evening service. The youths had other plans, mostly to attend the Sunday night movie at Granada Theatre. Sunday movies at the time were equated in our community with the certain downfall of youth.

"We'll go to church if you'll play 'Sweet Sue,'" one student chided Woods.

"I'll do it," the organist replied.

The student audience that evening was larger than usual, wondering how Woods would fulfill his promise.

Sure enough, while collection plates were being passed, the young people heard their request number, even though some of the older folks may have failed to notice "Sweet Sue" wasn't in the hymnal.

Even though the present student generation has musical and other preferences which differ from the older churchgoers, we can't fault the younger set on its performance at the University Presbyterian Church in Austin.

It was refreshing . . . hopeful . . . stimulating.

Presbyterians aren't much given to congregation-participation in a worship service, but the students had some clapping hands and joining in singing "what the world needs now is love, sweet love." This was the recessional.

The service was like a revival, which certainly the spirit of America can stand these days.

FOR WANT OF A TAILLIGHT REFLECTOR

I almost lost the war for want of a horseshoe nail.

Once a famous poem was written about the horse which lost a shoe because it lost a nail, and the horse then lost its rider which caused the loss of the battle.

In my case, it was a faithful 10-year-old Mercury automobile, a perfectly sound metal steed which flunked its safety inspection because of a lost taillight reflector.

Until then, I hadn't missed the reflector which is a small piece of a big taillight assembly. I don't know when or how it disappeared. The supervisor at the inspection station overlooked it too.

But this inspection took place the day the Department of Public Safety sleuth was checking the shop.

"Don't pass this one," he warned, probably using the motions of an umpire calling a batter out at the plate.

Mr. Krueger (nobody uses his first name) was the repair shop supervisor who carried all my automobile problems on his shoulders.

Krueger sadly informed me after a few hours that reflectors no longer were being made for the old Mercury. The dealer had none, and neither did the regional parts warehouse.

A search determined there was no Mercury Montego taillight intact at any of Austin's wrecking yards. A call went out over the national used parts teletype circuit. Nothing.

September turned into October, and my machine gathered dust on the repair parking lot. I thought of making a federal case of my problem. Call Col. Pat Speir at the DPS, or get the Legislature to pass a law. The problem is, they had already passed a law which grounded my Mercury.

I dared not drive the car. Austin police are diligent about enforcing the safety inspection law. One of the worst blots on my traffic record is an arrest for driving with a sticker that was three days expired. The lesson cost me $5, although I pleaded ignorance and pledged to remedy the oversight by having my car inspected the next morning.

While Krueger searched the nation for a reflector, I discovered that Austin has good bus service, if you don't mind walking a few blocks to the bus stop. It cost 15 cents to ride during off hours, and the walk helped firm up my midriff.

After more than a week, Krueger reported in our daily telephone conference that one of the mechanics would be going to the boondocks for the weekend, and that his father had an automobile graveyard which might contain the right model Mercury.

Then I left town for three days, and was overjoyed to learn that my car was ready. The new used taillight (had to buy the whole fixture) cost $48.08. The reflector probably cost 25 cents to manufacture.

Now I have three taillights, including the one with the missing reflector, which is carefully preserved in case it has some useful parts to fix future damage.

The whole system is rather silly—an example of America's

great throw-away economy. For lack of a two-bit piece of glass, a good automobile came near being junked. A comparable new car replacement probably would cost $10,000.

I'm old-fashioned, but modular mechanics should never replace the repairman who can fix things, not just replace them. The new system is wasteful.

Thankfully, the country is still blessed with competent craftsmen, but the number seems to be shrinking and many of the best ones have grown old.

He couldn't cope today, but the first automobile mechanic I ever knew was an ex-blacksmith named Ben Gardner. He could repair almost every part of the simple machinery of his day.

Ben kept Plainview's cars running. But after awhile, he bought two horses and moved to a cabin alongside a creek in Southern Colorado, far from traffic sounds.

There still are conscientious people serving the traveling public. One day, Mr. Francis Hill (operator of our neighborhood Exxon station) talked me out of buying new tires, although mine were four years and 25,000 miles old.

"You don't need any new tires," advised Mr. Hill, just as I was about to order four. "Your tires' tread is practically knee deep."

Oh, yes, since I started this, I do have a new rebuilt starter on the Mercury. The wrecker hauled old faithful back to the shop yesterday, but I was back on the street in four hours. It cost only $91.36.

WARTS — A COMMON DENOMINATOR

In the commotion over multibillion dollar health programs, we are happy to see somebody paying attention to the problem of the lowly wart.

This happened on page one of the *Wall Street Journal,* in a 14-paragraph in-depth article by John E. Cooney.

The subject has more universal appeal than even sex or religion.

Warts have been with us since the beginning of recorded

history, and apparently they are as much an engima today as they were to Adam and Eve.

Our personal recollection of warts begins the day an itinerant wart remover visited our West Texas town with an electric needle. Electricity had just been invented, possibly, and somehow this stranger got permission to remove a large wart from my leg, for pay. We remember neither the man's name nor his face, but to this day remember the odor of a burning wart, and also carry a scar the size of a dime.

Historically, warts are supposed to be bad. Ours have come and gone but we still have a few, including some in private places.

Like politics, warts happen to be a subject where everybody can claim expertise. Even a small child knows that handling toad frogs causes warts. But the most learned scientists have made little progress in the wart field.

While science fascinates us (we married a chemistry teacher), certainly education isn't much help in handling the wart problem. Our in-residence expert says "kunjooring" (spelled conjuring) warts is the best method of removing them, and she points to the success of an elderly, uneducated Negro woman who practiced the art at Temple many years ago.

While we do not know what a wart-conjuring entails, we can testify to the success of another primitive practice of the healing arts. (Note: This is not to discredit our fine medical profession, into which we graduated a son.)

A child in our family once had a stubborn fever that defied the skill of physicians and pharmacists for weeks. A middle-aged black maid volunteered to help. She sewed a postage-stamp sized cloth bag, filled it with salt, and tied it around the patient's neck.

The fever subsided to normal right away, and stayed there as long as the salt sack was worn. When the sack was removed, up went the fever. Apparently this treatment wore out whatever was causing the fever, for the patient is now grown and healthy and must have quit wearing the salt sack during that first summer.

This proves little except that the human is still primitive and superstitious, with a thin veneer of civilization and knowledge.

Warts likely will plague mankind forever, like weeds and hackberry trees.

DON'T VACUUM MY BOWL GAME

A vacuum cleaner almost broke up one long and happy marriage that we know of.

It happened on New Year's Day, which came close to being a marital disaster even though both parties involved had eaten plenty of black-eyed peas to insure good luck throughout the year.

The blow-up came when the wife turned on the vacuum sweeper while her husband was watching the fourth quarter of that exciting football game between Texas and Notre Dame in the Cotton Bowl.

The couple finally decided against instant divorce, since the lawyers were all busy watching the game too. But the incident does show the strain that TV football viewing has put upon the American household.

The lady who switched on the electric sweeper wasn't trying to start a family ruckus. She wasn't any big fan of Texas or Notre Dame football, but mainly New Year's Day was the first time she'd had to start cleaning the house from a round of holiday visiting from the kinfolks.

A whole new field of marital, legal, social, and even medical problems seems likely to arise from televising football. One couple we know struck a balance by purchasing ''his'' and ''hers'' television sets, which are kept in separate rooms. While he is watching the bowl games, wrestling, or whatever athletic event happens to appear on the tube, she relaxes with the afternoon soap opera relating the tear-jerking problems of the American family.

It is doubtful that the script writers can dream up situations which exceed the real-life tensions brought about by television viewing.

Just the other afternoon, a family crisis hit our household when a 6-year-old girl insisted on watching a Popeye cartoon just when an older relative (me) wanted to see the Rose Bowl game. The 6-year-old won the argument, supported by the other women who were present.

The television industry may little *reck* (correct) what a

strain it puts on the fabric of the American family relationship. Sociologists should look carefully into the situation, for it appears that new psychoses and new grounds for divorce may emerge.

What jury would convict a man for mayhem on the vacuum sweeper during the Texas-Notre Dame fourth quarter? If the defense was temporary insanity, wouldn't it apply to 73,000 who watched the game at the Cotton Bowl and millions out there in TV-land.

The football season is about over (as many citizens mutter "thank goodness"). But there is always politics coming along.

And when the candidates start crowding the screen a few months hence with their messages on how to save the republic, millions will wish they could watch a replay of the Cotton Bowl football game. Or even a repeat performance by the vacuum cleaner.

PLAIN WHITE SHIRTS

Christmas comes but once a year but buying a plain white shirt has become an adventure for all seasons.

We realized this truth anew while Christmas shopping for a young man who had plenty of snazzy bright-colored shirts with flowing collars and lacy cuffs. What he needed was a conventional white shirt, suitable for funerals and similar occasions, if not for wearing to Christmas dinner.

A well-known and fashionable downtown men's store, branch of one in Dallas, had rows and racks of shirts in rainbow colors and prices to match.

"A plain white shirt?" asked a clerk incredulously. "Let's see what we have."

This produced a "white on white" number, looking like three shades of white on a white background.

"—We don't want a shirt to wear with a tux," we said, "just an ordinary white business shirt."

"We don't carry those any more," said the clerk with a hint of hauteur after showing several other so-called white dress shirts which would be the very thing for somebody in show biz.

Prices were mostly $15 up. One $10 number looked like it was made by a dropout from shirtmaking school.

Down the street, we visited another large men's store whose counters were lined with noonday shoppers. Another weary middle-aged man argued with a young salesman, who had just sold him four gaudy colored shirts, a doubleknit suit with big lapels, and related haberdashery.

The customer still wanted a plain white shirt, just for old time's sake.

Out came the assortment of glittering whites with fancy collars and cuffs. The customer shrugged in disgust.

Our path to the exit was interrupted by an imposing-type woman.

''Can I do something for you?'' she inquired.

''Ma'am, all I wanted was a plain white dress shirt.''

''Long or short collar?''

''Short collar.''

''Plain or French cuffs?''

''Plain cuffs,'' came with a sigh of relief.

''Wait here,'' she whispered, ''I think we can accommodate you.''

Our new-found friend disappeared into the storeroom for 10 minutes, emerging with a beautiful, plain white shirt, cotton and polyester, short collar, plain cuffs. The price was reasonable.

Away went a very satisfied purchaser, clinging to his package. The victory may be the high point of our Christmas season.

And we can hardly wait for the January white (shirt) sales.

Good shopping and Merry Christmas, you-all.

LET THE SELLER BEWARE

You might say ''caveat emptor'' is dead.

The old Roman doctrine of ''let the buyer beware'' applied to manufacturing and merchandising for centuries.

Now the doctrine has gone the way of chariot racing.

Products liability is the hottest item in the damage-suit field, and it is a growing concern of those making, selling, and insuring the products.

The situation is much like medical malpractice damage suits, a legislative committee was told.

And like medical malpractice, the worry isn't so much over awards where the manufacturer or seller probably is at fault as in cases where his responsibility might reasonably have ended.

Hugh C. Yantis, then chairman of the State Board of Insurance, used a personal example. He displayed a small pocket-knife which he said he uses for many purposes other than cutting. Yantis uses the knife to bore holes in wood, and a couple of times cut his finger when the blade closed from this activity.

Should the manufacturer and seller be held liable because Yantis cut his finger?

Yantis didn't think so, even though knives can be made safer — and more expensive — by putting a lock to hold the blade open.

This is a small example of a large problem.

Ed Clay, a Dallas engineer and president of American Body and Equipment Co. of Grand Prairie, testified before a legislative products liability study committee:

"We can't know everything that happens to our product," said Clay. A purchaser may misuse, abuse, modify, or fail to maintain a product properly and still win a damage suit, he asserted.

Clay mentioned a man who sued for injuries when he tried to mow his hedge with a power lawnmower.

Yet there often are real grounds for seeking damages, and Americans long have been irritated over failure of some companies to make good on warranties or sell products which proved defective. The recall of automobiles for repair of defects discovered after the sale is a well-published problem.

Power equipment, chain saws, lawn mowers — modern equipment poses hazards never known to the Romans or even to citizens a generation or two ago. Americans are captives of manufactured products including gadgets.

Christmas toys long have been known to include gifts which are dangerous for children to use.

Witness Yantis offered the interesting theory that the rise of products liability lawsuits is a revolt against materialism.

Certainly it is part of a new consumer activism. It poses problems that threaten to get out of hand.

CREDIT EASY — BUT NOT CHEAP

A San Antonio bank where I never had any account once mailed me a book of personalized, printed checks along with an invitation to write checks whenever I wish.

This sounded like a great idea, and Morehead immediately started planning a no-expense trip around the world to be financed with checks written on our friendly San Antonio bank.

Reading of the fine print revealed, however, that the bank expected us to repay the money — at 18 per cent interest.

While it would be nice to write checks on a bank without depositing any money, the dream trip exploded with the information about the interest. I didn't want to borrow any money, especially from a bank in another city where I've never done business.

The San Antonio bank is headquarters for a credit card service to which we belong. We use the credit card, but don't borrow money on it.

Easy credit, regardless of the interest, seems attractive to most folks. Long ago, I learned a lesson as a country lad who wrote off for some greeting cards to be sold at a large profit.

The greeting cards were rather ordinary, and I quickly ran out of prospects after making sales to the immediate family and a few adult friends who couldn't say no.

Left with half my greeting card stock, the few dollars collected from sales dwindled away. I considered myself out of the greeting card business. A few weeks later came a letter demanding payment. I had no money left, not even enough to pay postage to return the remaining cards.

Next came a threatening letter announcing the matter was being turned over to the company's attorney.

An embarrassed, half-frightened youngster laid the problem on his parents. After a scolding on my lax business ability, my parents advanced the money to repay the debt. I'm sure they made me work it out.

Credit is a great thing, unless abused.

The practice of department stores, pharmacies, service stations — just about everybody in business — extending credit card loans bothers me. As a man with only a university education, it is difficult to ascertain when one is paying his account or borrowing unneeded money at high interest rates.

Awhile back, I mistakenly paid the wrong column on a pharmacy bill and the next month received a statement on how much interest and remaining principal was owed. Borrowing from a drugstore was the farthest thing from my plans, and I told them so. The next month, the company deducted the interest from my bill. Computerized bills can be tricky, and the customer must read carefully to find whether he's paying an account or obtaining a loan.

Computerized banking sounds like a great thing, but it has problems. When you hand the grocery checker your bank card, you may be paying 18 per cent interest on your potatoes.

A banker told me that many customers, large and small, are very skeptical about having payment deducted instantly by computer on a purchase.

The reason is, he explained, that ''floating'' checks is a great American custom. It lets the person have a few days to get to the bank with the money after writing a check. The nation's system of banking would break down if everybody had to pay in full immediately, our banker said.

That's probably the reason for the automatic loan credit card, which is rapidly turning American business into lenders.

NECKTIES . . . NOT FOR EVERYONE!

Good news was when narrow neckties were coming back into style.

Your writer was in the forefront of this fashion movement. We still have a full supply of narrow ties purchased when they were ''in'' some years ago.

We also have three sizes of black bow ties, bought at my wife's insistence that my black tie for tuxedo-wearing was out of date. Since the tux gets worn about once a year, styles change between wearings.

Give or take a few, we probably have 50 neckties acquired by gift, purchase, or inheritance. About half a dozen get worn to work or social occasions. I don't recall ever wearing out a necktie, and some are so old they were cleaned back when the laundry charged 10 cents per tie instead of a dollar.

Narrow ties are described as two inches or less wide. Included in my wardrobe are some late models up to four inches across, all gifts from women in the family. Since the statute of limitations has probably run out on being sued for ingratitude, I can truthfully report that I never did like wide neckties. They are like wearing vests around the neck.

Historically, neckties served a much more useful purpose than they do today. Three hundred years ago, cravats were introduced by Croatian mercenary troops. These neckpieces made of linen were worn partly to keep one's head from being separated from the shoulders by a sword.

The first cravats were ancestors of neckties, and merchants began selling to clothes dandies "a band or scarf of fine cloth often trimmed with lace formerly worn around the neck tied in a bow or knotted so the ends hang down in front." That's according to Webster's dictionary.

My neckties range from pencil-thin bolos to some that could be worn properly with a long-tailed morning coat to the Ascot races. I don't own a long-tailed coat, except an overcoat.

One "Indian" bolo on inspection turned out to have been made in Taiwan. But then we have an authentic Mexican shirt manufactured in Korea and purchased in San Antonio.

We don't care much for neckties, as you can tell by reading this far. Possibly this is due to some relative having been the guest of honor at a "necktie party" in the Old West.

The necktie is a bother. Texas climate wasn't made for neckties from March to November. Many men have eliminated neckties from business as well as informal wear. A distinguished appellate judge has confided that he has conducted court minus a necktie, but draped from collar to ankle in a flowing black robe.

"You'd be surprised what some judges wear underneath," he added.

A Miami Beach columnist once started a no-necktie crusade, and the city was visited by delegates from northern manufacturers threatening to withdraw their tourist business from Florida. The necktie won.

Hand-tied bows are just an exercise in frustration for a fellow with five thumbs on each hand.

Once an actor preparing to perform couldn't tie his bow tie, according to the story. A call went out to the audience for a volunteer who could tie a bow.

A spectator hustled backstage and offered his services. He told the actor to lie down.

"Why can't you tie it on me standing up?" the actor demanded.

"Because I'm an undertaker," came the reply.

JOHNNY CAN'T READ PAPERS

Newspapers and the public schools share a common problem of encouraging people, particularly young people, to read.

The American Press Institute (API), supported by the nation's newspapers, held a conference to discuss the problem. Participants made numerous suggestions which probably would increase the readership of newspapers, but none had much encouragement about overcoming the basic reason: television is diminishing the amount of reading done by Americans, virtually from kindergarten to the grave.

Accompanying this is a decline in reading ability among students from 5th grade through high school, according to David E. Wiley, an API speaker discussing test scores.

Wiley, an educator, concluded on a gloomy note:

"The high school graduates of today who are poor readers will continue to be poor readers. They have already gone through the system.

"And they are the next generation of parents."

Robert M. Stiff, editor of the St. Petersburg, Fla., *Independent,* explained the disturbing trend as follows:

"From ages 2 to 18, a child spends 17,500 hours sitting in the classroom and 18,000 hours sitting in front of a television set.

"Pre-schoolers spend an average of 54.3 hours per week watching television.

''The child is accustomed to color, a sense of motion, lots of big graphics, humor, and entertainment. He gets that with a simple push of a button in his living room.''

The newspaper isn't a dying industry, but its leaders are deeply concerned about how to keep their product informative, interesting, popular, and profitable.

Editor Stiff pointed out newspaper reading is a habit that, once established, usually lasts a lifetime. But fewer and fewer young persons are developing the habit, despite efforts of newspapers to appeal to what is perceived to be the youthful taste.

One bright spot is noted by Stiff: a Canadian seminar for teachers on ''Newspapers in the Classroom'' favors the newspaper over television ''in every positive category . . . '' and as a classroom teaching tool even where both mediums are available.

But Stiff said teachers, including young products of the television age, must be won over to newspapers because those without the newspaper reading habit usually prefer television.

The situation is far from hopeless. There will always be an important place for the printed word, for broadcasts are too fleeting and often oversimplify. Actually the mediums are not in full competition. Many television watchers read avidly the explanation of what they had seen previously. They can re-read and file the printed information if they wish, without any need for instant replays.

Some public school educators are getting as interested as publishers in the decline in reading skills and habits.

Schools have become too permissive. Education suffers, and hardly anybody is pleased with the result—least of all many high school graduates.

Dr. Benjamin Harris, professor of educational administration at the University of Texas, put it this way:

''Kids don't like what's going on in their schools, and it doesn't matter whether they are successful or unsuccessful students. ''. . . Maybe (the answer) is right in the schools in the way the teachers and administrators are running the educational process.

''We have philosophy in American education that argues if anything goes wrong, its the kids first . . . the parents second

. . . and we never get around to talking about the schools' responsibilities for failures . . .''

And maybe the big reason for the decline in newspaper reading among youth is simply that Johnny never learned to read.

III

Eggnog And Chitterlings

POP'S ANNUAL EGGNOG

"Take one fifth of Four Roses, minus one stiff drink . . ."

Thus begins a recipe for Pop's Eggnog, which is a Christmas tradition in the Morehead family.

With so many eggnog recipes around, we won't burden you with details of our family's. Besides, Pop's Eggnog was more a performance than just a recipe.

Prohibition still was abroad in the land during our boyhood, but somehow a bottle of Four Roses bourbon appeared in the Morehead household every Christmas on the dry West Texas Plains.

After stocking contents were examined and gifts unwrapped, our father went into his eggnog act. This always came close to breaking up the marriage with our mother, who was trying to bake a turkey, make fruit salad, and do other things in the kitchen for a big, wonderful dinner.

In good times and bad, our family always ate well, even when money was scarce. We lived on a dairy farm, and around us grew most of the ingredients for fine eggnog — all home-grown except for flavoring and spirits.

Mom could fix Christmas dinner for the whole family with less to-do than Pop took making eggnog. But after all, his was a once-a-year performance which nobody should forget. He's been gone several years, but Pop and eggnog remain almost synonymous in our family.

After testing the Four Roses to make sure the contents weren't just colored water, Pop "separated the eggs" — usually with sloppy assistance of the younger generation. Sometimes our mother came to the rescue to keep her kitchen from being

ruined completely by persons too inept to separate the whites and the yolks with an eggshell, dividing the result into two bowls.

This was accompanied by the Great Bowl Argument over what bowls to use. Nearly all bowls are too small for this purpose. We don't recall Pop ever making eggnog over the years without overflowing the bowl and still having part of the liquid left over.

Yolks were stirred and whites whipped. Sugar was added, along with pure cream and sometimes a little milk.

Pouring the Four Roses became a high point, with Mom always remonstrating that the nog would be too strong. Pop settled that argument by adding another splash of bourbon triumphantly.

The next strain on the family tie came in making space in the refrigerator — already full of Christmas goodies — to let a large bowl of eggnog "set." Good nog must season and chill. Ours was well sampled while fresh, but the real serving always took place later.

After losing the Refrigerator Space Shuffle, Mom won a victory by banishing the eggnog crew from the kitchen while she cleaned up the mess and got on with the dinner-fixing.

Children shared the exictement of eggnog-making then and now in the Morehead family. It is an experience to savor. Pop's is the best eggnog we know of, and we'll tip the good-tasting cup to the memory of one who established warm tradition in our family.

POP MOREHEAD'S EGG NOG RECIPE—2½ gallons

20 eggs separated (room temperature)
 1 quart whipping cream
⅔ pint sugar (Pop measured in pints and quarts except as
    follows):
⅕ gallon Four Roses bourbon ("less one stiff drink")
nutmeg

Beat egg whites until stiff (lean over bowl while smoking pipe — not really — although Pop was a constant pipesmoker)
Whip cream "like hell"
Beat yolks well on very slow speed

Add sugar, a couple of tablespoons at a time to the yolks, beating well after each addition

Pour whiskey VERY SLOWLY (this is most important) so as to cook the eggs. (Lean over bowl . . . smell mixture . . . swear eggs are not very fresh.)

Add whipping cream. Blend only, fold in. By now you need a dishpan to hold the mixture. Stop and find one.

Add stiff whites, small amounts at a time, saving some to put on top to blend with spatula.

Sample, exclaiming: ''By god! It suits me exactly.''

Nutmeg to taste. Serve to dry multitude.

(Note: a 25-egg mix (our family is non-conformist, including recipes) served by Pop's granddaughter, Judy Chapin, to 15 guests, had two quarts left over.)

GEORGE'S CHRISTMAS PROJECT

A Christmas that George Slaughter remembers best is the one when both sheep gave birth to lambs right there in the manger scene.

It wasn't on the program for the nativity exhibit which Slaughter sets up every Christmas at Good Shepherd Episcopal Church in West Austin. But the two baby lambs did add a nice touch.

This blessed event drew international attention when the news wire services reported it, and friendly letters came from all over.

The nativity scene at Windsor and Exposition is an annual labor of love for George and the good shepherds who participate. Slaughter has been doing it for more than 20 years. He spends one whole day gathering the livestock, over a 100-mile route. The exhibit runs from Dec. 21 through Christmas Eve, and each Christmas Day Slaughter spends another six or seven hours returning the animals and poultry to their owners.

In a typical year he borrowed a trailer at his sister's ranch near Dripping Springs, drove six miles to pick up a couple of sheep at Hardie Bowman's, then 18 miles to a stable that owns a pet burro named Eeyore, and called Don-keyote by some youngsters.

Eeyore is no ordinary animal. He was imported from England. Flew over in an airplane. George said Eoyore looks a good deal like the Mexican donkeys of the Southwest, with just a touch more class. The animal is named, of course, for the famous A. A. Milne donkey of children's books.

A dairy farm several miles distant provides a calf. Ducks and chickens are sometimes added as needed, as the recipes say.

This menagerie for four days and nights occupies a pen put up annually across the street from Good Shepherd Church. George and a couple of church employees put up the pen, complete with manger.

A doll is used for the manger-child, but the other characters are real. Five persons serve in one and one-half hour turns for each of two crews nightly. Some nights the weather is so bad the shepherds, Mary, and Joseph must use handwarmers as they stand beneath a plastic awning. Dozens of people participate in the scene during its 4-day run, as motorists and pedestrians stop to admire the exhibit.

For a few years, George doubled as a shepherd but now his assignment is only to gather the livestock.

He got into this project originally because the Slaughters live on a farm that 20 years ago was 10 miles from Austin but now borders the city limits. The only animals they have around home these days are pets, for George is busy managing a large meat processing plant and other properties as well as spending many hours in charitable activities.

One year a borrowed duck disappeared from the pen. The surmise was that some heathen filched the duck for Christmas dinner, but the bird reappeared two days later as mysteriously as it had departed.

One reason we mention George Slaughter and his Christmas project, is that at that season many persons turn thoughts toward things spiritual and good-hearted.

George does it the year around. The phrase ''let George do it'' could have been coined for our friend Slaughter. He spends a lot of time every month in church and civic work, because he thinks it is important. The Slaughters are an old family in Austin and have long given freely of themselves to make this a better community.

While others of us take Christmas Day off, after dinner is eaten and the gifts opened at the Slaughter household, George hitches up the trailer and drives to Good Shepherd to return the nativity livestock to their owners.

He sometimes needs some help with Eeyore, George said, because the donkey is more than a 1-man loading job.

DOVES AND TAXES—SIGNS OF SPRING

One of our white doves laid an egg.

Carroll Abbott issued a new wildflower newsletter.

And my hair is thinner from the annual trauma of preparing an income tax report.

These are signs of spring, which has been bursting out around Texas.

The redbuds are spectacular. So were the lacy wild plum blossoms.

A wonderful thing about spring is that no two are alike. Some wildflowers bloom profusely one year and disappear the next, with another variety decorating the landscape.

First, back to the white dove. My wife purchased two from our granddaughter, rather than see them sold to strangers. Within a few weeks, one egg lay broken in the bottom of the cage. Some small sticks were put in the cage, and the doves made a nest. Another small pearly egg was laid there.

The pair of doves, I'm told, takes turns setting on the nest. (Note: a bird "sits" on a perch, and "sets" on a nest.) Since the pair seems identical (except to each other), I can never tell which is warming the egg.

The cooing of doves, mornings and evenings, is a wondrous sound. Ours live in a large cage out-of-doors, and cooing permeates the neighborhood. It also attracts cats.

One morning, another visitor arrived. It was an Inca dove, smaller than a mourning dove but marked similarly. The Inca apparently responded to our doves. Inca doves live around Austin, especially inside the city.

Meanwhile, Mr. Wildflower — Carroll Abbott — distributed his harbinger of spring, a newsletter about wild Texas plants. Abbott is the state's lone full-time collector of wildflower seed, which he sells to nature lovers.

Our sun-tanned friend, also a literary man, bore a press release reminding that Texas has no single ''state flower.''

The bluebonnet is so designated, but at least three varieties of bluebonnets grow in the state, and the Legislature has labeled all three ''official'' flowers. And if any other lupines are found, they'll be ''state flowers'' too.

Abbott included the intelligence that the late John N. (Cactus Jack) Garner got his nickname in 1901, as a state legislator from Uvalde, trying to designate the prickly pear as state flower. The bluebonnet(s) won.

Garner later became a noted speaker of Congress and vice-president, but never achieved the presidency. So the famed Texan had at least two disappointments in his life.

A reminder that even springtime has its drawbacks is the April 15 deadline for income-tax paying.

While I am working up the figures, my wife plugs her ears, and the birds stop cooing. Neighborhood dogs and cats avoid the premises.

A tax lawyer predicted the ''reform'' act passed by Congress will become known as the ''tax lawyers relief act'' because it will provide them with so much business.

Sen. Lloyd Bentsen of Texas added:

''. . . the taxes people pay are enough of a burden without forcing them to hire a lawyer or accountant to learn how much they owe.''

Bentsen said early-filled returns (mostly for rebates) show 11.5 per cent—or more than two million returns—contain errors.

The senator said even the ''simple'' short form contains 50 blanks to be filled out, and requires the citizen to add, subtract, calculate percentages, and multiply. Bentsen asked Congress to simplify the forms.

Meanwhile, how about making the accurate completion of a typical income tax return a requirement for graduating from high school? This will be a practical test of public education.

TELESCOPE BIRTHDAYS INTO ONE

After a weekend of celebrating family birthdays, and mine coming up, I concluded that what this country needs is a single birthday each year.

Let everybody observe the whole family's birthdays at the same time, then leave the whole business alone for another year.

There's no reason we can't have flexible birthday celebrations. For example, we observe Christmas Dec. 25, although the experts say Jesus Christ was probably born at some other date. It's as good a day to celebrate the event as any.

The once-a-year central birthday which I propose would be some distance from Christmas, perhaps in mid-year, to get it away from the significance of the holidays with all the gift-giving. Besides, it would give everybody at least twice a year to be eligible for gifts.

I have always felt sorry for children born around Christmas, because for the remainder of their lives there will be a tendency of prospective gift givers to combine the two, and really knock the person out of the second occasion.

My own birthday is close enough to Christmas, five and a half weeks.

For years, the date posed a special problem, however. Nov. 16 formerly was the opening day of the deer, turkey, and quail-hunting season, and your correspondent often was away in the woods when my wife wanted me home to eat cake.

In my wife's family birthdays have always been a major event, the occasion for much family gathering and merriment. It became even more major when our granddaughter was born on my wife's birthday, Sept. 27.

Both our children were born Nov. 9, three years apart, another cause for big doings.

Their mother starts planning the next birthday celebration immediately after each one is finished.

With all our relatives, remembering birthdays would be a lot easier if everybody observed the same date. We could buy greeting cards, or presents, in bulk.

Hopefully, nobody would be overlooked.

Race horses all have Jan. 1 as their official birthday for purposes of deciding their racing age. I've never heard a horse complain about this, although a horse born on Jan. 1 might actually be running against one born 364 days later on Dec. 31, if I understand the system.

Some people will hate me for suggesting a single birthday for the whole population. Some employers let the worker off on his/her birthday. This wouldn't necessarily be halted by the Morehead birthday plan, for it could be scheduled for a work day every year.

The whole holiday system is getting more structured, anyway! Most folks love the 3-day holidays which come up nearly every month. This allows more time to get worn out and broke before getting back to their jobs. You can be as blue on Tuesday as on Monday, if you work at playing hard enough.

When *The Dallas Morning News* established a 5-day working week, some years ago, replacing six days, one older colleague considered it almost immoral to take off two days a week. He believed in the work ethic, but he didn't get much support around the office.

Our friend did make one concession to the new order. He came to the office on Saturdays without his necktie.

My birthday plan may fail to catch on because of the horoscope situation. If all humans were Scorpios, as I am, think what a creepy planet this would be. Occasionally, I check the horoscope to see how the forecast matched what really happened. It seldom does. But when the forecaster hits, it worries me that somebody knew before I did what was going to happen to me this day.

If we cannot celebrate a single birthday, at least a person should get local option to change birthdays if he wishes. Freedom of choice is a basic human right.

CHITLIN' TIME DOWN SOUTH

The arrival of wintry weather serves to remind country folks that it's hog-killing time again, and with it, chitlin' time.

Chitterlings (pronounced chitlins) are a Southern delicacy

made from hogs and recipes are passed from parent to child, mostly among black citizens.

Roy McCarthur of the Austin Headliner Club staff kindly provided a recipe for chitterlings. Since none of the cooks around our house has been willing to try the dish, our appetite is unsatisfied.

But informed opinion is that chitlins is (are) nectar for the gods, if you like nectar. A plump black woman in line at the supermarket carried a 10-pound container of chitterlings, which she said her husband and four sturdy sons could devour at a single meal, when cooked. Further, she invited us to dine the next Tuesday at a department store lunchroom where she cooks, because it was ''soul food day'' with chitlins. Unfortunately, we never made it.

Chitterlings are a pig's small intestine. Mexicans make a somewhat similar delicacy called menudo from the insides of a goat or other animal. Europeans serve tripe made from the stomach of cattle.

Our recipe comes from the *Soul Food Cookbook* courtesy of the aforesaid Roy McCarthur and his family.

The recipe:

Eight pounds of chitterlings.
Water
Two medium onions, sliced
One lemon, sliced
Three cloves of garlic, crushed
One teaspoon salt
One teaspoon pepper
One-half teaspoon allspice
One-half teaspoon whole cloves
One-fourth teaspoon thyme
Two bay leaves
One-half cup chopped parsley
One-fourth cup white vinegar
One-fourth cup tomato sauce.

Soul Food Cookbook says to soak the chitterlings in water overnight, then wash them very well, turn inside out and remove excess fat. Place in a large kettle and add water to cover. Add all the ingredients except tomato sauce. Simmer until the chitterlings are tender. During the last 15 or 20 minutes of cooking, add the tomato sauce.

Chittlings can also be fried. For this, omit the vinegar and tomato sauce and drain when tender. Cut into 2-inch strips, dip in batter or roll in flour, and fry in deep fat. This serves eight to 10.

Chitterling cooks advise the mixture gives off a powerful aroma. One adviser said this can be overcome by adding a little baking soda while cooking.

We also have a recipe for frying chitlins: four pounds of cooked chitterlings, three eggs beaten for dip, rolled in cracker crumbs with salt and pepper and deep-fried.

Chitlins weren't common in West Texas during our time there. But we did kill hogs when the first norther arrived, and made a delicious fried morsel called cracklings which now grace cocktail parties as hors d'oeuvres. Cracklings are mostly scraps from pork rinds after the fat has been rendered into oil through heating. Cooled, the oil becomes lard. And the cracklings become delicious just as soon as they are cool enough to eat.

—And, smack your lips over cracklin' bread.

NEVER FOOL WITH AN APRIL FOOL

April Fool is a good label for a month when bad and good things get so confused.

Take some of our experiences one April day.

Item: Accidentally, our elderly automobile was stolen . . . and returned.

Item: A Dallas lady opposing Daylight Saving Time wrote a nice fan letter. But she mistook me for a State Representative.

Item: We bought 40 cents worth of "staples," plainly marked on the sack, to repair a wire fence 75 miles up the country. When we arrived at the fence, the bag contained roofing nails.

Item: It hailed on our house.

All of these mishaps had happy endings.

The Great Auto Theft occurred one evening at a neighborhood restaurant where we dined with out-of-town friends. What an empty feeling it was to find our faithful black sedan missing from its parking place when we were ready to leave. We couldn't remember its license number and fumbled a few minutes before calling the police.

While struggling with this problem, aided by the restaurant management, our car pulled up outside. A most embarrassed couple got out. Their automobile of identical model and color was parked also at the restaurant and they sent a friend to fetch it. Their key started our car. The couple was soon horrified to discover it wasn't their machine they were driving. And we were happy to get it back.

It was back home for the Big Hail. A few dents in the automobile prove that.

Even a hailstorm had a satisfactory aftermath. First, this area badly needed the rain. Also, the insurance company was punctual about putting an adjuster on the roof, reporting a total loss, and sending us a check to cover the repairs, less $100 deductible.

A competent retired roofer, who still works for old customers, responded promptly to a call for help, and the roof was replaced within a week at a reasonable cost. Now we need more rain, minus the hail.

The Dallas lady's letter about Daylight Savings Time was addressed "Richard Morehead, Texas Legislature." About a week after being postmarked in Dallas, it reached us with the notation "Not a Member Any more." Perhaps this comes under the heading of good news. In fact, I never was a member and could never get elected.

Our scant fan mail included recently a letter from Dallas calling us stupid, so possibly that is one vote we would not get. But the balance of bouquets to brickbats is very nice, thank you.

April must be a happy month, even with the Legislature in session and the dry winds blowing. The wistaria, roses, and azaleas still managed to make a pretty showing. The Hill Country Bluebonnet Trail will attract thousands on Easter weekend. It is a beautiful trip.

Easter isn't for pessimists. Neither is Central Texas in April.

NO HOLIDAY IF YOU'RE NOT WORKING

While you working people are out there pleasuring your-
selves during the Labor Day holiday, shed a tear for those retired
to a supposedly-permanent vacation.

There's something to be said for the privilege of just turning over in bed and going back to sleep any morning you wish,
as most over-the-hill former employees can do.

But this is different from the good old days when you sa-
vored the prospect of an upcoming 3-day holiday or a whole vacation. The fun is gone from shaving a couple of hours from
work on Friday afternoons to get away on rest and recreation,
and you can't drag back to a paying job on Monday morning explaining the joy of getting sunburned.

Like some other activity, you can get farther behind about
taking a vacation and catch up quicker than you ever imagined.
Don't everybody speak at once, but who really wants to be off
work full time?

Once we had a drinking uncle who claimed he had a holiday for every day in the week, hence the reason to celebrate and
abstain from supporting his family.

An old Southern gentleman on the other side of the family, whose working career consisted of two years as a justice of the
peace (he lived to be 90), explained that ''the war'' of 1861-
1865 wiped out his expected livelihood from inheriting a plantation in Mississippi. He never adjusted to working for money. It
was the delight of numerous grandchildren for whom he had
plenty of story-telling time.

Lest any reader weep because I must sweat over a hot typewriter while others are out playing games, forget it. I wrote this
column one day, expecting to be sitting beside a pond at Gravel
Hill on Labor Day waiting for doves to fly by. Friends in the
company gave me a fine Browning .20 gauge shotgun as a retirement gift and this will be my first chance to use it except for
practice.

Although retirement gives you less need for an alarm clock
and a calendar, there's a lot to be said for it.

We have more time for family and friends. More time for

each other. More time for reading. More time for cleaning out
the closets and storeroom. This takes a lot longer than one might
expect when you stop to read something you wrote 20 years ago.
Right now I'm working on a 1965 copy of *Newsweek,* mainly
trying to find out why I saved that issue.

And the working folks who are free to travel only on weekends some day will find it more pleasant to take your trips on
week days when there's less traffic and fewer hell-for-leather
drivers trying to make it across Texas between meals.

There's a sort of Parkinson's Law about retirement: Any
task can be expanded to fill up any given amount of time.

You can take longer than before, and perhaps even do a
better job. Or if the mood strikes, take a nap. That's what some
of you Labor Day weekenders wish you could do Tuesday, unless
you sleep at your desks.

One reason it is easy for a writer to ''retire'' — which he
never really does — is that nobody ever knows when he's working. Many a person has gone through an entire lifetime without
much effort, just telling people he is ''writing a book.'' It is a
genteel way of loafing.

Wick Fowler, a talented writer, never found another subject that excited his interest like covering World War II. So Wick
spent the remainder of his life looking for something interesting
to do, and writing occasionally. He was on this newspaper's pay-
roll for years, and just called in if he didn't decide to come to
work on a given day. He'd give some excuse such as ''the creek is
up,'' which satisfied the management even if it might have gotten another person fired.

Wick paid little attention to Labor Day, the holiday honoring workmen.

''Nobody ever knows when I am working or when I'm
off,'' Wick used to say. ''Sometimes I think I ought to wear an
arm band to show when I'm on the job.''

IV

Weather, Water And Oil — Texas Style

WOOD STOVE WOES

The winter is almost gone and I am still barely speaking to Wood Stove. For almost a decade, faithful Wood Stove and I enjoyed a cordial relationship. We took good care of each other.

But something happened. Wood Stove began belching smoke all through the inside of the modest cabin which we enjoy sometimes at Gravel Hill Ranch.

Without warning, Wood Stove started coughing a horrid-smelling substance shortly after we'd loaded it up with nice pieces of green live oak during a norther.

Our clothing, curtains, even the dishes soon smelled like they'd been dipped in creosote.

After several hours of this torture, while I kept hoping the little 2-hole iron heater would soon start behaving, I carried the smoking embers in a coal bucket into a pasture where they were left to perish in a cactus patch.

Next I tried an old never fail fire-making recipe, better even than the Boy Scouts know. I filled the stove with twisted pages from *The Dallas Morning News* and added some dry kindling saved in a garbage can for just such an emergency.

Drafts open, I poured half a cup of kerosene onto the wood and struck a match.

Kerosene and nauseous newspaper smoke poured all through the house, with nothing coming out the chimney. Naturally, I cried. Smoke filled my eyes. My bride shouted from the bedroom: ''Open the doors before we suffocate!''

The blizzard blowing outside quickly blew most of the smoke from the house, while dropping temperature inside to 42 degrees. Smoke still filtered from every crack in our stove.

As soon as I could see again, the glowing remains were

shoveled into the coal bucket and carried outside, where a good fire soon blazed in the coal bucket. This went into another cactus patch.

Hair and clothing sure smell icky after being smoked with kerosene and newsprint.

After two hours sulking in a cold cabin, I determined to try again. Dry cedar. Nothing burns better than dry cedar. Into the back yard armed with an ax, I split a pile of old cedar stumps. They split easily, almost exploding. These were so dry they could be burned in a rainstorm.

Back to the kitchen with an armload of freshly split aged cedar. First, twisted paper. Sticks of cedar, a dash of kerosene.

"You're wasting your time," commented my wife, who considered wrapping herself in our electric blanket. "Something has stopped up the chimney. Maybe dirt daubers." (These little black, wasp-like insects build nests of mud all over the place.)

"At least, everything will smell better," I replied. "Nothing beats the odor of cedar smoke."

A match was struck. The paper smoldered. Smoke leaked from every crack in Wood Stove. Cedar smoke, by the way, irritates the eyes as much as green oak or pages from *The Dallas Morning News*.

The whole cabin filled with smoke. Open the doors. Raise the windows. Back to the old coal bucket. Out with the smoking cedar and paper. Another nice fire for the cactus.

After a brief spell of breathing outside air, we called off the whole project, vowing to take down the chimney next summer to see what went wrong.

The next day, our fortunes improved. Bob and Virginia Bain drove out from Austin. I related my problem to them.

Bain is a handy fellow, left-handed. He inspected the stove pipe from the yard and announced it was stopped up near the top, which has a little tin hat to keep out the larger birds and animals.

Bain insisted we fix it. So we located a 30-foot ladder. Bob climbed to the chimney top, against my better judgment, and removed the top section of pipe.

"Here's your problem," he announced victoriously.

''Your strainer is stopped up.''

Resin from the first green oak smoke had coated the screen wire which we inserted last summer to keep out the woodpeckers, which were the subject of an earlier essay.

Within 15 minutes, Bain had replaced the screen wire with larger mesh hardware cloth, and restored the whole thing.

Inside, we built a small fire of twisted newspaper. By then it was too warm to need a whole fire. Smoke rushed quickly up the chimney to the outside air.

It was like announcing election of a new Pope.

DAYLIGHT SAVING STEALS AN HOUR

''Why shouldn't Texas go on Daylight Saving Time?'' asked the Little Woman, selecting a subject for our daily breakfast table debate.

''—for one thing, I'd have to get up an hour earlier,'' came the reply.

''You could come home an hour earlier in the evening.''

A. ''I'm not a clock-watcher. It wouldn't work that way.''

Texas should get in step with the rest of the country, she insisted.

''What about El Paso? It would still be on different time.''

''El Paso will always be different,'' she said.

''Why should they make US change?'' I asked. ''Why not pass a law putting the whole country on Central Standard Time?''

''I'm for uniform time,'' she said. ''I don't care what they call it.''

''Suppose somebody sent up a clarifying amendment to the Legislature's anti-Daylight Time bill, putting the whole United States on Central Standard Time?''

''Now, you're getting silly,'' she said. ''What we need is Uniform Time so it will be the same time all over the world.''

''You mean I might have to get up and go to work in the middle of the night?''

''Exactly,'' she said, passing an article titled ''One World, One Bedtime?'' from a newsletter to high school science teachers and students.

Science and Math Weekly printed the views of Sidney Sternberg, vice-president, Federal Systems Electro-Optical Systems Inc. concerning how worldwide universal time might be achieved.

Beside this program, the Texas Legislature's argument over Daylight Saving Time seems puny.

Within the lifetime of persons under 35, Mr. Sternberg predicts, time zones will be eliminated. Instant communication and the ability to travel from any city in the world to any other city in a maximum of an hour and a half will make the 24 existing time zones too old-fashioned to exist, he said.

The proposed installation of uniform world-wide time would be upsetting at first, the author admits. People accustomed to going to bed in the evening and arising at dawn would be disoriented at first by having to reverse the process in some cases. So Sternberg proposed giving everybody the first week in January as a vacation, when the new system takes effect, so they can adjust to the change, just as a jet traveler sometimes must take a few days presently to get readjusted from a fast air trip through several time zones in which a whole night's darkness may be lost.

The key to the Sternberg revision would be to shorten every day by four minutes, making a 23 hour and 56 minute day. This would make an extra day every year, which would be observed as Feb. 29, except every fourth year there would be a Feb. 30. The present calendar provides for an extra day every ''leap year.''

By speeding up clocks four minutes a day (Sternberg said this already happens to his wrist watch), everybody's hours would work out during the year to have as much exposure to the daytime sun as they did previously.

In fact, says Sternberg, there would be more daylight leisure time than under present circumstances.

Although the farmer's rooster might crow at 1 a.m. under this system, Sternberg predicts it would be a boon to stockbrokers and broadcasters, and a benefit to the average citizen—after he got accustomed to it.

TEXAS WEATHER — ICE AND FOAM

J. Frank Dobie told a story which illustrates well how quickly Texas weather can change.

A South Texas cowboy saw a "blue norther" approaching and headed his horse for the home corral at full gallop.

"When he arrived, the front of the horse was covered with foam, and the rear end covered with ice," said the famed folklorist.

It is difficult to be satisfied with Texas weather. Last August, we wished for cool weather to end the days of over 100-degree heat. Now, Texans are ready for the snow and ice to let up.

Comes now disturbing, conflicting news from two experts predicting the climate (1) is going to get colder in the future and (2) it is going to heat up. Take your pick.

The warmer-weather prediction came at the American Astronomical Society's Convention on the University of Texas campus.

Dr. Bert Rust, a consultant for Union Carbide Corporation's Nuclear Division, said the increasing build-up of gas carbon dioxide in the atmosphere leads scientists to believe the next 100 years will see average temperatures rise by two to five degrees Fahrenheit.

While shivering citizens now may think a warming trend would be fine, Dr. Rust said such a long term change in the world's climate could bring disaster. Fertile grain-growing areas could become deserts, polar ice caps would melt, and ocean levels would rise to inundate coastlines and coastal cities.

Erle Stanley Gardner, the noted mystery writer, told us of the two drunks aboard ship who got concerned about the prospect of the polar ice caps melting.

"—And it would bring water pouring right through the portholes of our ship," one reasoned. So they took another drink.

They would be reassured by the recent dispatch from Antarctica, home of the South Pole, from a Dr. George Denton of the University of Maine, who should be an expert on cold weather. Dr. Denton predicts the earth is going to become colder, which would be just as upsetting as heating up the old sphere.

Meanwhile, West Texans are wishing it would rain and East Texans wish it would stop. One thing we can be sure of: Texas weather can change rapidly.

Our annual rainfall is 25 inches a year,'' said one old-timer. ''And I was here the night we got it.''

Floods often follow droughts. Californians suffered from a severe water shortage in 1976 and 1977, which brought about rationing in places. It has been raining and snowing almost without let-up in the Pacific coast state for the past month or so, and residents there are ready for some dry weather.

We have no particularly favorite weather. When the sun shines regularly, for example, dry-land farmers usually wish it would rain. We grew up in a dry land farming country, where a mature native once remarked, ''I've spent my whole life waiting for it to rain.''

Autumn is our favorite season, because it brings beautiful colors and what the British call ''fine'' weather—clear and cool. Summer is the worst season in Central Texas. Humans should hibernate in late summer around here to avoid exercising.

Springtime is the favorite of many persons, perhaps most. The grass greens and the flowers bloom after the drabness of winter. The land comes to life again in the spring, but to the office worker, it usually brings an attack of spring fever, wishing he was outside in the sunshine.

ENERGY SHORTAGE

Once everybody laughed when an energy expert testified ''I'd buy a good sweater'' when asked what to do about upcoming winter. Later, the President of the United States wore a sweater and long underwear as part of his clothing on a visit to frozen Pittsburgh, to survey the effect of the severe cold.

Nobody laughs now about the predictions, made repeatedly in past years by informed persons in the oil and gas industry, that the country was on a collision course between supply and demand for energy. Most citizens apparently didn't believe the predictions. The collision occurred.

The effect is shaking the halls of Congress, American industry, agriculture . . . the whole economy. This may even become known as the winter that changed the American lifestyle of the past quarter-century, just as it has made its impact on winter apparel. News reports say most stores are sold out of long underwear.

From Congressman Jim Wright's remarks here, this reporter gathered that the reality of this monumental problem is just hitting Washington. There has been a growing awareness of it in other parts of the country, starting in the producing areas of the Southwest.

The Fort Worth congressman, who is No. 2 man in the U.S. House of Representatives, spoke of "12 to 26 years" of oil and gas reserves in the country. This is longer than forecast down here where the stuff is produced.

Gov. Dolph Briscoe gave "8 to 10 years" as the life of presently-known reserves at current prices. The removal of price controls would increase the "recoverable reserves" immediately through simple economics. There's a lot of oil and some gas underground which cannot be produced profitably at current prices. It isn't being hoarded by the owners. They can't afford to lose money producing it.

But the main problem is America has increased its fuel consumption so rapidly that something must give. The nation simply doesn't have enough oil and gas for immediate needs at any price.

Forty per cent of U.S. oil is imported. We are at the mercy of higher-priced Middle East and South American producers. Another boycott would be much more disastrous than when the filling stations were running out of gasoline. We are much more dependent on foreign oil now than then.

Besides sweaters and long underwear, Americans must become accustomed to using less energy — colder homes in winter and warmer ones in summer . . . less space cooled and heated. The use of natural gas for boiler fuel must be stopped all over the country, as the Railroad Commission has been doing in

Texas on a phase-out program for nearly two years.

Many Americans lived comfortably before the country went on such a splurge of energy consumption after World War II. They will learn to do it again.

MODEL A FORD IN A CRISIS

The model "A" Ford which our former postman, A. E. Krause, drives around Austin should give the experts an idea of how to ease the energy crisis. Somebody should re-invent the Model A.

We remember the excitement in 1928, a prosperous year just before the Depression, when Henry Ford presented his new wonder machine, successor to the Model "T" which made Ford famous. Ford dealers all over the country kept their first Model A under wraps, standing in showrooms covered with bedsheets until the appointed day of unveiling. It was big national news, and well should be.

Krause bought his Model A second hand in 1931, after it had been purchased new three years earlier for $485. He has driven it for years and done most of the repair work himself. For several years he drove a paper route as well as being a mailman.

A touring car, no longer manufactured, his is a sleek-looking 4-door which seats four or five adults comfortably. It also has running boards, which long ago disappeared from the motoring scene. These provide steps into the car, or even a place to stand if someone wanted to ride outside on the running board instead of inside, as daring youth often preferred.

Although Krause isn't wealthy, he has declined offers to trade it for a new Ford or for $5,000 cash.

The Ford gets around 20 miles to the gallon on highways, but doesn't go out of town much any more. It has been 143,000 miles, with the original ignition brushes. Its clutch and top have been replaced, but otherwise the machine runs virtually as it came from the factory, except for tires and the need of a paint job.

Since a touring car has no side windows, there's no need for air conditioning, which wasn't invented until many years later. It has a gear shift and standard transmission.

Any old-timer is thrilled to watch Krause in his vintage Ford roll smoothly to a stop with 4-wheel brakes beside a new sports car of some youthful driver. And the Krause Ford is likely to be first away when the traffic light turns green.

Americans have added increasingly to their transportation costs and energy consumption by air conditioning, automatic transmissions, power seats and windows, and dozens of lesser gadgets which are nice but not necessary.

Henry Ford proved in 1928 that automobiles can be built to last. The Model A is comfortable, and it is fast. We had a used one during our final year at the University of Texas, and can report that it would have no trouble keeping up with the modern cars violating the 55-mile speed limit. Even on hump-backed 2-lane highways of yesteryear, the Model A cruised at 70 or above if you could hold it on the road.

The Model A has 21-inch wheels, compared to 13 to 15 inches on current models. Krause buys tires from mail order houses.

Gasoline in the 1930s cost 15 to 20¢ a gallon and generally wasn't as good as refineries made in the 1970s. The ''hottest'' gasoline of the 1930s and the cheapest was so-called ''drip gas'' from the East Texas oil field, a highly flammable but unstable mixture collected from pipe-lining oil.

Something also went out of motoring with emergence of the ''closed car'' — those with windows all around and solid tips.

My father once owned a touring car, which we sometimes drove along dirt roads with the top down, a rather dusty experience. Once my brother and I — both small boys — took turns throwing our hats at the back seat, claiming the wind was blowing them away. A wise man, Pop, decided after awhile to let us walk back and get the hats instead of backing the car. That surely stopped the wind from blowing our hats away again.

CYCLONE CELLARS

Years ago folks called them cyclones, and nearly every rural residence had a ''cyclone cellar.'' Fortunately, we never needed a cyclone cellar because the Moreheads never had such a hole in the ground. But we visited many a cyclone cellar, and really found little to recommend them unless one wanted to hide from a storm or maybe the law.

Weather experts today refer to such storms as "tornadoes" or the bigger ones in the Gulf of Mexico become hurricanes. Cyclones are those black funnel clouds that dip from the crashing thunderstorms such as visit many Texas areas.

The old cyclone cellar was about six feet deep, with a ventilation chimney sticking above the mound of earth that covered the pit. Usually it was about six feet wide and 10 feet long. A flat, or nearly flat, wooden door opened onto the stairs where one entered the creepy, damp inside. With the door closed, cyclone cellars were always pitch dark inside, and coal oil (kerosene) lanterns were the "emergency lights." These gave off bad odors and possibly deadly gases.

Some West Texans called them "dugouts" although we always considered a dugout to be a habitation dug back into a hillside, a sort of boarded-up cave which had plenty of natural insulation.

Storm cellars always seemed to be about as dangerous in calm weather as in cyclones. They were the natural dwelling place of spiders, probably poisonous, and of small ugly greenish salamanders with yellow spots that were called "waterdogs" for their love of damp places. They were said to be harmless, but their appearance was frightening.

Some cellars served a dual purpose. Shelves were installed to store homecanned fruits and vegetables, and sometimes items like potatoes and apples. These were the deluxe cellars, always cool in summer and never freezing in winter.

Texas Tech University has published a pamphlet, academically titled "In-residence shelters from Extreme Winds." This is a sort of modern version of the cyclone cellar, although it doesn't usually require any digging. Actually, it is a small room near the center of a house, constructed of materials which will withstand strong winds, falling timbers, and such flying missiles as rafters blown free from the roof.

Tech engineers say such quarters are too expensive to use for a whole house, but they are safe havens in a storm. Air space at the bottom of doors is suggested, or vents for folks who fear suffocation. The engineers recommend masonry construction, such as concrete walls, and steel-reinforced doors.

In the post-World War II nuclear attack scares, several of our friends and relatives built bomb fallout shelters. Some were pretty plush, large enough for the whole neighborhood, and equipped with supplies of water, food, flashlights, and portable toilets. A few even had liquor cabinets!

None of these has actually been used as a bomb shelter, but they made interesting conversation pieces when first built. One relative on the South Plains built a bomb shelter in the basement, and it gets occasional use during tornado alerts.

We wonder if there are more tornadoes than formerly, or whether the reporting is better. Visitors from other states often stay scared just from hearing the evening weather reports in summer and fall.

Two tornadoes are in our background. While I attended the University of Missouri, a cyclone did considerable damage on campus. I slept cozily in a rooming house during the entire excitement which didn't seem any different than our regular South Plains weather.

The next time, I watched a big black cloud envelop our old home place, a dairy farm. I didn't know it was a cyclone, but after it passed the roof was missing from the big barn, scattered over a mile of prairie. A Jersey bull hit by a slab of debris was the maddest bull you ever saw.

MY BROTHER'S FEET WERE COLD

One sharp recollection of the winters of our boyhood is my brother's icy feet. We slept in an unheated upstairs bedroom in a farmhouse on the plains of Northwest Texas, where temperatures drop below zero during blizzards.

Going to bed on a freezing night — at least being the first person in bed — was an experience not unlike bathing among the ice floes. One mild remedy was to heat an iron or a brick on the back of the "base burner" stove which burned coal transported 2,000 miles from Pennsylvania.

The hot iron or brick would be wrapped in a towel and inserted at the foot of the bed under the covers. This worked fairly well to warm the feet unless one kicked off the towel cover and burned his toes.

Before the invention of the electric blanket and insulated sleeping bag, family arguments developed over who had to insert himself between cold bedsheets first.

At our house, only the kitchen, breakfast nook, and "back living room" were heated regularly during the winter. Five other rooms remained refrigerated by the weather except for the occasional use of a portable "coal oil" (kerosene) heater to break the chill.

All fuel was shipped to West Texas from other states — bituminous (soft) coal from Colorado for cooking, and cleaner-burning anthracite (hard) coal from Pennsylvania for the big pot-bellied heating stove with its smoky yellow windows, isinglass, made from mica.

During winter storms, a trip to the snow-covered coal pile was very stimulating. Black coal dug from beneath fluffy white snow was cold, wet, and dirty when carried into the house in coal buckets. A few small pieces usually spilled onto the floor, a hazard later to bare feet.

Unlike more fortunate areas, there is no firewood on the Texas Plains. Pioneers sometimes burned dry buffalo or cow "chips," earning the region a reputation of being a place "where wind draws the water and cows chop the wood."

Being near the greatest gas field discovered in the nation in the late 1920s, the giant Panhandle field, our country was among the first to make the great leap forward from coal to natural gas. Gas also was used to generate electricity.

Texas officials emphasize what even few Texans realize: Texas isn't just the biggest producer of oil and gas in the United States, it is also the biggest consumer. To an unusual extent, Texas' economy is based on oil and gas. Until the Arabs take it away, Houston ranks as the biggest city based on petroleum, with Dallas not far behind.

Increased federal taxes on oil and natural gas would hit

Texas harder than any other state, notwithstanding the anguish being voiced by New England citizens who grew accustomed to cheap oil and gas from Texas and the Middle East.

Compared to bringing coal to Texas from Pennsylvania, the higher-priced oil and gas is still a bargain. We have been fortunate this past half century to possess plenty of oil and gas in Texas. But the supply isn't unlimited or nearly as free like the wind. Oil and gas reservoirs are expensive to find and are depletable.

Our concern is for what happens to Texas as its own production becomes scarce.

ECOLOGY MACHINE OF THE FUTURE

For years, I have had this developing romance with windmills.

The television set in our family living room is topped by a miniature windmill and tank, made of horseshoe nails welded together by an Amarillo artist.

Above this ornament hangs my favorite painting, featuring our country cabin and windmill. Here Ficklen, the former *Dallas Morning News* cartoonist and a fine artist, did the painting.

Windmills have belonged to our family all my life. They have pumped our water and provided a comfortable sound in the rural landscape. They must build the creaks into windmills, for I never heard one that didn't creak when it was in action.

Now windmills loom large in the energy future, with some experts predicting they may generate as much as 25 percent of all U.S. electricity. Windpower has provided electricity in some remote areas for years, and the interest in wind energy is rising in proportion to the prices utilities must pay for gas, oil, and coal-lignite to run conventional generators.

Hopefully, all this won't spoil the image of windmills. Some of the experimental generators are funny looking, more like something from outer space than the West Texas Plains.

Probably the new windmills will break down like modern air conditioners and automobiles, which the old mills seldom did, if kept greased and turned off during freezes.

Occasionally, a windmill loses a slat or two in a cyclone, but usually it keeps on pumping water until it falls down from neglect, which takes a long time.

Our latest windmill in the Hill Country is an Aermotor. We don't know its age, but the final addition was a storage tank with ''1926'' scrawled in the wet concrete.

A few years ago, when our Aermotor was more than 50 years old, it required a service call. It threw out all the bearings from the turning axis and scattered them for 50 feet around in the grass and weeds below. The big wheel stood at a crazy angle and wouldn't budge. Wendell, the local windmill fixer, was summoned.

We never found all the bearings for the axis, and new ones couldn't be bought. So Wendell restored the ones we could find on the ground and got the water to pumping again. We have also replaced the leathers for the pumping valve and rusted pipe from the hole, plus a worn-out sucker rod, a long wooden rod that helps pump the water.

Windmill mechanics are scarce and said to be more temperamental than artists. They work when and where they choose. Wendell climbed the flimsy ladder up our windmill tower to the nearly non-existent platform on top. He called for tools by shouting to an assistant on the ground, who flung the requested wrench more than 30 feet into the air where Wendell caught it. Considering how many deaths and injuries have resulted from falling off windmill towers, this is real bravery.

Recently, our windmill has again developed sounds like it is coming apart whenever the wind direction changes. It may require major surgery.

The Aermotor people still make windmills in Arkansas, although for awhile it was considered impossible to buy new windmills or even parts made in the United States. Maybe we will buy a whole new windmill to prepare for the fuel and water shortages forecast in the future. The manufacturer's advertisement is appealing:

''No monthly power bill, no line cost, no embargoes, no air pollution. No wonder windmills are known as the ecological machine of the century.''

If everybody gets into windmills, it could cause problems, says a scientist friend with a semi-straight face.

''Don't put windmills too close together,'' he advises. ''They could use up all the wind.''

Between growing up in West Texas and spending most of our news writing career around the Texas legislature, I'm convinced this country will never run short on wind. It may blow unevenly, such as tornadoes, but there's enough, if it is just spread around.

Thankfully, new windmills are rising on the Texas landscape. Few wind generators are in use yet, but the research is going full blast and success will follow. Wind power has been used for years to generate electricity for isolated customers, but until recently the cost and technology favored other energy sources. This is changing. One widely discussed prospect is for wind generators to be linked to conventional utility lines and buy from the utility when wind supply is inadequate. When wind-made electricity becomes excess, it could be sold back to the utility.

IT ISN'T CHEAP TO SAVE WATER

A great woman we knew set an example of water conservation that Texans would do well to follow always.

Our neighbor, Mrs. R. L. Ligon, saved water meticulously even when it was plentiful. When she washed vegetables, the water then went on her house plants. Not a cupful was wasted.

Mrs. Ligon and her husband pioneered in North Texas-Southern Oklahoma before the Wichita Falls region had enough population to be noticed for its hot, dry summers. But they learned early that water is life itself and never should be wasted.

A blistering summer and drought reminds city dwellers as well as country folk of the importance of water. Several communities in the Austin area sometimes are forced to ration because of inadequate water supplies or mechanical breakdowns.

It may be a portent for the future of this fast-growing state, for long-range planners predict water may become more critical than energy in the years ahead.

Fortunately, thought is being given to the problem by

some people, usually from necessity.

A La Quinta Motor Inn opened at College Station has the nation's first water reuse system in the hotel industry.

The 114-unit facility had reduced water demand and wastewater volume by more than half, according to Texas A&M's Water Resources Institute. The city water system was unable to handle any greater volume, so the La Quinta people chose innovative conservation rather than move to a less desirable location.

All water from 114 sinks and showers is piped into underground tanks, with total capacity of 40,000 gallons. This so-called ''gray water'' is filtered and disinfected with chlorine, then piped to the laundry where 500 pounds of towels and sheets are laundered daily. The laundry wastewater goes back into the tanks for re-treatment, then is colored, scented, and piped to the rooms for use in flushing toilets, as well as watering outside plants.

The system has had problems, such as freezing once in winter, and adjustments were made to cope with algae, clogged filters, and valves.

It isn't cheap, for La Quinta invested more than $100,000 in the project, but its water bill is about one-third that normally paid by a similar-sized motel.

The manager receives few complaints. The reaction of most guests is ''that's a good idea,'' says manager Charles Shaddox.

Fortunately, most of Texas still has ample water for normal human use even in droughts, but it is doubtful this will continue much longer because of the influx of people and the increase in per capita water usage.

Because of strong recurring droughts and usual hot summers, Texas has some water development advocates even though resistance has been strong from environmentalists in recent years.

A major concern about water is that it takes too long to overcome a shortage after the well or reservoir runs dry.

West Texas, part of the world's breadbasket of grain and cotton production, for a quarter century had been trying to promote interest in bringing water from other states, and/or transferring surplus water from East to West Texas. The import idea is very much alive. Surplus water would be brought from Arkansas or rivers which periodically flood in the Middle West.

Without such aid, irrigation from underground sources in Northwest Texas will disappear for the most part, and the cost will be paid by grocery buyers all over the country. The loss also will be tragic in less fortunate foreign lands where surplus American grain has been a lifesaver, although inadequate to keep up with the booming world population.

WHEELIN' AND DEALIN' IN OIL

Walter Cline of Wichita Falls wanted to bury for all time the old rumor that drillers often find oil, but keep the discovery a secret. "You hear it and you hear it, but it's simply not true," said Cline.

The former Wichita Falls mayor ought to know. He drilled wells for major and independent operators for forty years. "Nobody ever hinted or suggested to me that we do anything except get oil when we stuck a bit in the ground," said Cline.

Cline's views on this and other oil topics are kept on record — literally — at the University of Texas Library in Austin. It's part of a project, paid for by an anonymous Texan, to keep for the future the word-of-mouth recollections of old-time oilmen. Men still alive helped bring in the first wells of Texas' vast oil industry. Their generation is passing fast. Some have died since they were interviewed.

With tape recorders, Mody Boatright and his assistants helped these pioneers record what happened in the early Texas oil game. These stories come from the mouths of drillers and leasehounds, scouts and producers, bankers and lawyers, roughnecks, and tool-pushers, businessmen and peace officers.

No search for statistics, the goal is to preserve flesh-and-blood accounts of the birth of Texas' oil industry. It is not a history of million-dollar deals.

The object is to capture such memories as the day an East Texan got even with a friend who was snooping around a "tight" well. The place was fenced off to keep outsiders from learning what success, if any, the drillers were having. When the friend got inside the fence, the driller asked him to step a little closer to inspect the machinery. When the intruder stepped within range, a bucket of slush from the derrick "accidentally" poured over him. Just the driller's way of letting the fellow know he was unwelcome.

One reel tells how Claude Witherspoon, later living on a ranch near Dilley, helped discover oil at Corsicana in 1894. The crew was drilling a water well for the state orphans home. Instead, they struck oil. It gushed up the hole and ran into the street. The water drillers didn't know what to do with an oil well. But from this accidental start, the Texas oil industry grew. Leasing got under way around Corsicana. Rotary rigs were brought in.

In 1901, Witherspoon went to Beaumont for the Spindletop boom, riding from Corsicana in his first railroad "sleeper." The Spindletop discover was made in January, but the boom didn't get under way until April, Witherspoon recalled. Business moved more slowly in those days.

More than fifty persons have been interviewed by Boatright and his helpers. The assistants were W. A. Owens, ex-Texan and ex-SMU student now at Columbia University, and Carl Wallace, oil editor of the Tyler *Courier-Journal.*

Several hundred others are listed for interviews, if the money holds out. Funds so far have come from the person, but other donations are expected. The idea came from Miss Winnie Allen, University of Texas archivist, during the fiftieth anniversary celebration of Spindletop field at Beaumont.

Recording is a fairly new way of preserving history. John A. Lomax used it to collect folk ballads for the Library of Congress. The words of great men in political history are being recorded in a Columbia University research project.

Boatright's interest in oil people dates back many years. He has written much about Gib Morgan, a real-life Texas oil-field character who can almost match Paul Bunyan. Morgan claims he drilled a well in West Texas with cable tools, using tanks for surface casing, and putting smaller and smaller casing as the hole became deeper. Morgan wound up drilling with a needle — he said.

The records tell about Sour Lake, Ranger, Burkburnett, Electra, Eastland, Batson, Borger, Goose Creek, East Texas, Luling, Mexia, Yates, and other fields.

Already interviewed are men like Walter Fair and H.P. Nichols of Tyler; B.J. Harper and Will R. Wilson Sr. of Dallas; I.T. Kent, J.S. Simkins, and Carlton D. Speed of Corsicana. All were associated with early oil booms.

Interviews include E. DeGolyer, B.H. Stephens, B.E. Hull, and several others from Dallas.

Wichita Falls' Driller Cline sets a philosophical pace for the series. Oil brings out the best or the worst in folks, he said. A good, honest church-going man who strikes it rich will put his wealth to worthwhile causes, as many Texas oilmen have done. He mentioned John G. Hardin, the former Wichita Falls man who gave away millions to Texas colleges.

A fellow who was a small-time stinker before striking oil usually just becomes a rich stinker, Cline added. "He shows up in the lobby of some big hotel all dressed up like a sore thumb and grinning like a jackass in a briar patch, and with a blonde on his arm," Cline describes this fellow.

When folks get rich, he explained, they just carry on with what they always wanted to do if they had just had money enough.

REPORTER'S LIFE CAN BE RISKY

Sam Kinch Jr.'s harrowing experience on a hijacked plane to Cuba dramatizes the hazards of newspaper work. The public is well acquainted with the risks faced by police, firemen, and men in the armed forces. News reporting may be less risky than some other professions, but we feel the public little realizes the difficulties and even dangers encountered in so mundane an event as covering a political campaign.

Much of the risk has to do with travel. Until the skyjack craze, commercial airlines were the safest way to go. But much travel by reporters and candidates in political campaigns is done in small private planes and bad weather. Automobiles too are unsafe at any speed when the driver is weary and the weather is bad.

Any session of reporters or candidates can produce a multitude of true tales about hairy experiences on the campaign trail. In retrospect, these bring laughter. But there's nothing funny about the two congressmen and two other men being killed in Alaska while on a campaign flight. Other prominent figures have died the same way.

One problem with campaign travel is that Texas politics hits peaks in spring and fall when the seasonal weather cycles produce storms. Candidates feel their schedules must be kept, almost regardless of weather, so they may haul the news gatherers along when the commercial aircraft wouldn't be traveling.

This doesn't count such inconveniences as occurred when a private plane hired to pick up a candidate and his party in Tyler turned back to Houston without landing because the warning lights showed its wheels wouldn't come down into place. The plane ultimately made a safe landing back in Houston, and the party had to summon — at high cost — a rented jet from Dallas to carry the candidate to the next stop.

Four times during our newspaper career, we've been aboard aircraft which ''lost an engine'' — meaning turned off in the air. In each case, fortunately, the planes had more than one engine so the planes managed to make safe landings. This also accounts for our aversion to flying in single-engine aircraft.

We also have been exposed five times to tear gas in the line of duty — the Democratic national convention in 1968, the Republican covention in 1972, and at other times covering racial rights demonstrations. Other reporters encounter similar experiences covering the news. It is a stimulating job but often very hard on the human anatomy.

Sometimes, reporters eat and drink sumptuously, but there's many a case of indigestion from gulping down a cold hotdog when there isn't opportunity for eating a decent meal.

Sam Kinch Jr. chose news reporting because he likes to be where the action is. The same motivates about everybody in the business. Sometimes the action is more than enough — such as Kinch's experience of flying from Houston to Havana with a gunman's pistol pointed at his head.

The first thing Kinch did after getting back was to file his great eyewitness story from Miami. A waiting staff of editors in Dallas got it into print posthaste — a truly memorable newspaper operation.

And the next day Kinch flew to California to join a candidate. He did stop long enough to assure his wife and family he was all right, except bone-tired.

COOKING WITH CACTUS

Several centuries late, we have discovered cactus cooking. Cactus salad was on the Morehead menu last week. It's good. And the salad will be better later this year when we can harvest some nopalitos (tender new leaves) from our resident prickly pears.

My first experience with cactus was unpleasant, but it had nothing to do with eating. Years ago in West Texas, a horse pitched me into a clump of prickly pear, and I harvested thorns from my backside for days.

Experts in the cactus-eating field use the new growth on the flat ''nopal.'' We'll talk separately about eating the cactus fruit, ''tuna'' in Spanish and ''pear'' or ''apple'' in English.

My wife, an innovative type, got into cactus all by herself. She harvested a few of the big leaves, tediously extracted the spines with a paring knife, then boiled the leaves for 20 minutes in salt water. Sliced, the cactus looks like string beans. The old leaves have a tough outer skin but a tasty, soft jelly-like inside. New young leaves are easier to prepare, and the embryo whiskers can be scraped off with a knife.

Discussing cactus eating is an experience similar to revealing an exotic ailment, which you discover everybody else already has survived.

The fact that cactus is a lifesaver to thirsty desert travelers is well-known, although some varieties of cactus are much better than others for this. The prickly pear grows in damper than desert climates, and is sometimes a nuisance, sometimes a livesaver for cattle raisers. Cattle often are kept from starving when pastures are exhausted by burning the spines off prickly pear and feeding the cactus to cattle.

One problem is that some cattle become addicted to cactus and will eat the plant, sharp points and all, with consequent disaster to their digestive systems.

Many South Texas deer are cactus-eaters, and some are said to get all the moisture they need from the plant without ever drinking water. Latin Americans long have eaten cactus in a variety of ways (and drunk some very exciting beverages therefrom). Doubtless the Indians who inhabited the western world before the white man arrived also ate cactus.

Luther Burbank, the great California plant breeder, developed spineless cactus but some of his reverted to their sticky old selves after a while. Cactus candy is a popular delicacy in Mexico and other places. Nopalitos are marketed in many Texas stores where Mexican-Americans buy groceries.

Our library includes ''Cooking and Curing With Mexican Herbs'' by Dolores L. Latárre, published here by Encino Press. Its recipes include prickly pear leaves in tomato sauce, prickly pear leaves with shrimp, and how to clean and eat the rich purplish-red fruit of the prickly pear. Hint: first hold the fruit with tongs under running water, brush off the pesky small stickers, and dry in a paper towel. The fruit should be peeled before eating.

In San Luís Potosí, Mexico, the prickly pear is widely cultivated for food, especially on remote ranches where fresh fruit and vegetables are scarce.

I also have a recipe for a nopalitos omelette, which I haven't tried. Once in Mexico City, I ate ''huevos rancheros'' (ranch eggs with pepper sauce). The dish almost burned out my bearings.

ARTIST CAPTURES PLAINS

Paul Crume would have loved Michael Frary's ''Impressions of the Texas Panhandle.'' The late, great plainsman of ''Big D'' column fame wrote beautifully about the short-grass country of Northwest Texas, which strangers sometimes mistake for semi-desert.

Michael Frary, a California-born University of Texas artist,

has captured the special character and charm of the Plains, ir-
rigated farms, canyons, ranches, cities, and people, both in
words and with paintbrush.

Frank Wardlaw, then director of the Texas A&M Press, per-
suaded Frary to write the book as a memorial to Loula Grace
Erdman, a Panhandle writer who died while preparing a book
on the subject Frary completed. The Paris-educated artist con-
fessed being quite skeptical over the assignment, but a close-up
of the Panhandle-Plains made him a true believer.

Primarily an artist first educated as an architect, Frary's
"Texas Panhandle" descriptive writing equals his brilliant
brushwork.

"Today, thousands of travelers go through the Panhandle
on 6-lane highways wondering, as I formerly did, if they will
reach Tucumcari by nightfall, or indeed if they will ever get out
of Texas," Frary concluded. "They should spend a night under
the sky in the Palo Duro. Then, when they listen to the stars and
dream about the Comanches and the buffalo, the early settlers,
and the Longhorns, they too will begin to know the Panhandle
and feel the raw essence of the land. It is a stirring and magical
experience."

Frary's paintings include horses and cattle, windmills, and
oil pumpjacks. "Autumn birds near Muleshoe" would thrill
late colleague Crume. Thousands of small birds hover over
maturing fields of grain against a seemingly-endless blue sky
dappled with fleecy clouds.

Crume wrote of his years "in the Lariat country" which includes Muleshoe, a town whose very name seems laughable to
outlanders.

"Muleshoe, to me, has become a special typical small
town," wrote Frary. "With a population of less than 5,000, it is
a center for marketing and shipping agricultural products. The
first two or three times I went through it I thought 'How could
anyone choose to live in this dry, desolate place?' Now I go out
of my way to revisit it. The Panhandle spirit exists at Muleshoe.
The people have a sense of humor. They call their town The
Pearl of the Prairie.

"They have erected a full-size statue of a mule in

downtown Muleshoe. The people have faught hard; they probably wouldn't leave Muleshoe for a place on the French Riviera.''

To Frary, the Texas Panhandle is one place where people remain unique. The men and women there, he said, ''have had to develop strong wills and stubborn attitudes.

''They are 'ornery.' This has resulted in a basic conservatism, a strong resistance to change. For the most part, the people of the Panhandle whom I have come to know, are honest, sturdy, friendly, set in their ways, with a surprising sense of humor and fierce pride in their land.''

This made me think of J. Evetts Haley, another old friend, a great historian of the Panhandle-Plains, a rawhide cattleman and scholar all at the same time. Haley's convictions about freedom from government regulations are well known.

Frary was impressed by ''fragile sunrises and flaring sunsets'' and the ''incredible flatness'' of a county where one can often see from one town to another. The tall grain elevators in smaller towns and the 30-story bank buildings in Amarillo became landmarks to Frary as to others who travel the Plains.

Michael Frary, a newcomer, has written and painted what persons from the High Plains have known all along but had difficulty explaining to others.

PROPER ENGLISH AND WRITERS

When George Sessions Perry was flunking freshman English for the third time, his teacher at Purdue University told him:

''Mr. Perry, I predict you will become a successful writer some day, but you will never pass freshman English.''

I found this one of the most interesting passages in Frank Driskill's book *Free the North Wind* published by the Eakin Press of Burnet.

Driskill, best known in recent years for being active in Texas political campaigns, may be surprised that I chose this over his comments in later chapters about Texas politics.

Before getting into government and politics, Driskill

coached high school football, taught economics at Texas A&M and for many years represented Macmillan Publishing Co. in Texas.

He brings a salesman's viewpoint into book writing and publishing in a very interesting manner.

Perry, of Rockdale, became a distinguished writer of books and articles for national magazines before ill health and other problems caused his death at 46 in 1956. He flunked first-year university English at Southwestern in Georgetown and the University of Houston before giving up the effort at Purdue.

At Southwestern, Perry found something more valuable to him than a passing grade in English. It was Claire Hodges, who became his wife, spelling coach, and editor.

Perry's published works were in the style of Mark Twain and John Steinbeck, humor against a background of poor and earthy folks whom he knew well.

Although Perry became widely traveled, his books reflect his upbringing in rural Texas.

John Mason Brown wrote the foreword to a reprint in 1959 of two of Perry's few books: *Walls Rise Up* and *Hold Autumn in Your Hand*.

"To imagine him without her (wife Claire) as a published writer is impossible," Brown said.

Perry regularly misspelled even simple words, which Claire always corrected in the manuscript.

Back to Driskill's experience with authors:

"The worst writers I have come in contact with in creative writing have been English teachers," he wrote. "Their material is usually correct in form and style, but it is dead and uninteresting."

"There are exceptions, of course. At Louisiana State University, two outstanding English teachers had the ability to turn out scholarly work but also a popular style pleasing to the layman. Cleanth Brooks and Robert Penn Warren put the university on the map by establishing the *Southern Review of Literature* . . . Warren is the only person I know who has won Pulitzer prizes in both prose and poetry."

Lest the reader think this writer believes students shouldn't bother about learning English, not so. English is the world's basic language, and certainly every young person in the United States needs to learn how to speak and write it well. Faulty communication is one of society's greatest problems, for it breeds misunderstanding.

Yet Driskill, admitting he's no great shakes as a speller, makes a valid point about English teachers, judging from some I had while in school. One or two were excellent teachers, partly because they knew how to instill in students an appreciation for good writing and reading. I learned much from Shakespeare, but very little from memorizing Chaucer.

Likewise, my university teachers almost uniformly disliked newspaper and popular magazine writing, and belittled short-sentence, short-word composition as the *Reader's Digest* helped to make popular.

Perhaps I am missing something, but about the only modern writer who ever sends me to the dictionary is William Buckley, and he might just as well use more simple words.

My English teachers did instill a fear of splitting infinitives (''to briefly state''), dangling prepositions (''what are little girls made of?''), the comma blunder (which I just made).

MAKE NO BONES ABOUT IT

Know what it means to ''hit the nail on the head''?
Make no bones about it?
It's all Greek to you?
Well, if brains were dynamite you couldn't blow your nose.
Now don't get offended, readers, the above are just examples of how Walter E. Long of Austin made a new game of old sayings.

A 1965 story in *The Dallas Morning News* related how Walter Long, a then retired business man, was busy preserving history. A dozen publications — limited to 1,000 copies each — were written by Long. None was ever sold by him, but sometimes he gave a few copies for a charitable organization to sell.

His ''Old Sayings'' in reality is a second-edition. So many people sent in their favorite old sayings after the first edition appeared that Long got out a larger volume. It included 80 daily game-lessons on the meaning of such phrases as those used at the beginning of this article.

"Hit the nail on the head," of course, means "Correct answer or diagnosis."

"Make no bones about it" is an old way of being "very plain spoken."

"All Greek" means that you can't understand what's being said. And the reference to brains and dynamite by now should be self-explanatory.

One couple sent Long 132 old sayings, most of them useable, when they found out he was collecting same into lessons. Dozens of friends have contributed one or more.

Long listed them into 80 lists of 25 sayings each, and suggested that men, women, and children play the game by writing down what they think each saying means. The correct answers are in the back of the book. The author recommended attempting to answer only one list per day, and he said there is remarkable agreement among the participants on what they understand the phrases to mean.

What child wouldn't know the meaning of "Slow as Christmas"?

Few of them would understand this old-timer: "Don't try to teach your grandmother to milk mice." That translates "don't try to advise your elders."

Many old sayings relate to animals:
Bright-eyed and bushy-tailed. (feeling great)
Scarce as hen's teeth. (a hen has no teeth)
A bird in the hand's worth two in the bush.
Make a mountain out of a mole hill. (exaggerate)
In a pig's eye. (foolish)
Frog strangler and trash mover. (heavy rain)
Booze hound. (heavy drinker)
Knee high to a duck. (short)
Slick as an eel.
Three shakes of a lamb's tail. (quickly)
Stubborn as a mule.

Fractious as a filly. (like a frisky girl)
Lost my rabbit's foot. (unlucky)
Wild goose chase. (fruitless)
Horse sense.
Happy as a chipmunk.
Quiet as a mouse.
Strong as an ox.

Some of the sayings doubtless go back to man's beginnings, in whatever tongue. Others are right out of Shakepeare: "Something's rotten in the State of Denmark."

Yet these colorful descriptions seem timeless. The astronauts have discovered that "once in a blue moon" men can travel in space, although at times it is "touch and go." A youngster who can relate 50 years hence the dramatic evens of America's space men doubtless will be dubbed "a chip off the old block."

Making your own list of descriptive phases, said Walter Long, is a good way to occupy one's mind while in the hospital, a doctor's waiting room, on a lonely ranch, or traveling. It becomes a fascinating mental exercise as well as a link with the past.

PECANS, A STATE PROBLEM

Our friend Jack Maguire once wrote a paean to the pecan which deserves further comment.

We know that Maguire, director of the Institute of Texan Cultures in San Antonio, is a pecan freak. Year-around we keep a bowl of pecans and a nutcracker conveniently located in the center of our house, knowing that when Maguire passes this way he will need to refuel on pecans.

All writers must make a living some way, but Maguire goes too far in his hymn of praise to the pecan, even if it is the official Texas nut. A pecan tree's place is in a field or orchard somewhere, not around human habitation.

After resettling in Austin from the treeless plains of West Texas some years ago, we were delighted when pecan trees planted by squirrels sprang up all around our place. Although we have eliminated several pecan trees to get some breathing

space, we still are surrounded by them. Pecan trees drip sticky sap on the automobiles parked in our driveways, both spring and fall. Twigs and even limbs fall on the house and the environs, including our neighbor's roof.

The squirrels work night and day, eating the trees' first tender buds in springtime and continuing until the last nut is safely tucked away in our back yard flower bed.

Although we live more than two blocks from the neighborhood park, squirrels can make the round trip to our residence without touching the ground, so thick are trees. Squirrels are cute little creatures but one can get over-squirreled. They bombard the roof with pecan shells and even green pecans. It isn't that we dislike pecans and squirrels. They have their place . . . not too close to the house.

The pecan industry has been mechanized by the big producers. Mechanical tree shakers have replaced the workers with cane poles and wagon sheets to catch the fallen pecans. Pecans are being shelled by machines, I'm told, although one hardly sees how this can work on the hard-shelled natives which have the sweetest meat and are preferred by commercial bakers and candy-makers.

The Legislature designated the pecan as the state tree in 1919, 13 years after the death of former Governor Hogg, who asked that a pecan tree be planted on his grave in Austin (also a walnut tree). Pecans grow in nearly two-thirds of Texas' counties and bring several million dollars a year to producers.

Texas has other trees which I think are prettier and would be just as suitable as the pecan for an official tree. Included are oak trees, especially the Spanish oak in its magnificent fall colors.

The mesquite is a graceful tree which grows nearly everywhere in Texas and has the character like that attributed to the rugged outdoor Texan. Incidentally, the mesquite also produces a nutritious bean. Deer and other wildlife, plus domestic livestock, devour the high-protein beans quickly.

We are not anti-pecan. Hogg may be right. But at the University of Texas Barker History Center we saw the (oak) office chair used by Hogg as governor. It was about half-again wider than the regular office chair, possibly the result of the oversize governor eating so many pecans.

This is one of our problems. Most of our favorite foods are fattening. We eat pecans, fresh or roasted, also peanuts, popcorn, etc. If we stopped there, we would be all right. But this is an addition to our regular meals.

Once on a trip, we met a Kansas farmer. He was Wally Latimer, still farming at 98 and he appeared on the Johnny Carson show as an example of longevity. Wally, a small man who weighs about 125, told us the mainstay of his diet is nuts, almost any kind of nut, eaten at every meal. Wally is agile as a squirrel, perhaps from eating nuts. Bad habits? Wally said he used to smoke a cigar every day, but he gave that up about 25 years ago.

So excuse me while I go into the yard to see if I can salvage some pecans from the pesky squirrels here. They're good eating, but the squirrels are good judges of pecans. The ones they discard are the worst ones.

DUST, DEPRESSION, AND COLLEGE

It is easier to understand Ronald Reagan, knowing he attended Eureka College in Illinois, at least it is easier for those of us who attended small colleges in the 1930s.

Mine was Wayland Baptist College in Plainview, and the description of Reagan's alma mater fits it.

Writing in the *Wall Street Journal* of ''Reagan's Roots,'' reporter James M. Perry related the presidential candidate's academic background.

Democrat Jimmy Carter attended the U.S. Naval Academy some years later, but Eureka educated Reagan. Reagan majored in sociology and minored in economics. The same professor taught both subjects. His economics views were traditional rather than later theories which have gotten the U.S. government and economy into a financial mess.

About 250 students attended Eureka with Reagan, half the number now attending the still-struggling Christian college near Peoria.

Such experiences influence one's life. Fortunately perhaps, most Americans attending college today have more money and less austerity. Yet Reagan considers his years at Eureka among the finest of his life.

Out on the West Texas plains, Wayland struggled to bring higher education and culture. It later became a 4-year institution and now has about 1,300 students.

In the early 1930s, Wayland had 10 faculty members and fewer than 200 students. The tuition was $50 per term, but the business office didn't expect all students to pay that much money in advance. Some paid in hams, eggs, vegetables, or chickens for the dormitory table.

This situation resulted from the fact in September 1931 the last of Plainview's three banks closed its doors. The town of 8,500 was forced to a cash and barter economy.

Wayland enrolled its first students in 1910 and like many other small colleges spent most of its life in financial straits. Many closed soon after they opened. Others survived to become strong private colleges like Southern Methodist, Texas Christian, Baylor, Rice, Austin College at Sherman, and Southwestern.

Significantly, figures show increasing enrollment, at least in Texas private colleges and universities.

They usually represent the vision of a few dedicated people.

At Wayland, the heroes were President George W. McDonald, his wife-teacher, and a tiny faculty that refused to leave when the bank failure took all of Wayland's money except $800 just when a new 1931 term was about to start.

The trustees voted to close Wayland since it was without visible means of support.

President McDonald rejected the action. Instead, he called the 10 faculty members together and proposed to keep classes going with whatever funds came in. The teachers would divide what remained after paying the monthly bills for utilities and other necessities.

One month, the faculty received only $32 each.

Reagan's years at Eureka College may not make him a better president than if he attended a more prestigious university, but he doubtless learned the basics at such a place, and we could well spread that around the country.

WHO FIRED THAT CANNON?

A band of University of Texas students "borrowed" two cannons from the State Capitol grounds, rolled them to the campus, and rattled windows of the Main Building with cannonfire in defiance of the president's wishes.

The students, mostly bushy-haired and several wearing mustaches, proceeded to oust the university president from his own bathroom and escorted him to face the student body in front of the Main Building.

Sound like today's news? Maybe, but this happened 72 years ago.

The last survivor of the episode — which has become a day of commemoration for University of Texas alumni around the world — was James W. McClendon, who retired as chief justice of the Third Court of Civil Appeals.

Except for automobiles, youth hasn't changed much between that day and this, Judge McClendon believed.

The law students involved in the cannon-firing of 1897 became conservative lawyers and sedate judges. One who successfully cautioned his colleagues to stay within the rules was Morris Shepperd, later a U.S. senator.

Dr. George T. Winston, a new president of the university, came here from North Carolina without full appreciation of Texas history and tradition. When students sought to declare a holiday on March 2, anniversary of Texas revolutionaries declaring independence from Mexico in 1836, Dr. Winston declined.

So McClendon's law classmates went into action.

They borrowed the two cannons from the Capitol grounds (with permission of state authorities, McClendon recalls). These were wheeled by hand to the university campus more than half a mile away on the afternoon of March 1.

Before the firing commenced, Morris Shepperd suggested that it would be a violation to shoot cannons on the "Forty Acres" without permission of school officials. So the students moved their cannons across the street to the athletic field, a site now occupied by Gregory Gymnasium.

The demonstrators discovered then that someone (later

found to be President Winston) had spiked their guns during the night, so they wouldn't fire. The students sent for a blacksmith. The field pieces were muzzle-loaded and fired, with tremendous effect.

"We rattled every window in the Main Building," McClendon recalls with a chuckle. "By the time we fired the second round, the whole student body came out to watch."

The cannon crew ran out of powder, and a new supply was delivered from downtown.

President Winston, seeking peace and quiet, sent word that if the students would cease fire "We can all celebrate in front of the Main Building at 2 p.m."

The students agreed. But Dr. Winston was missing at the appointed hour. So a "committee" including McClendon went to the president's home near the campus to fetch him.

"He was in the bathroom," McClendon said. "The committee forcefully dragged President Winston out."

Dr. Winston proved to be a good sport about it all. The president appeared (dressed) before the student body. Called on to speak, he responded.

"I was born in a land of liberty, nursed on the bottle of liberty, rocked in the cradle of liberty, and grew up a son of liberty. But the students of the University of Texas take more liberties than anybody I ever knew!"

V

Folks Worth Ridin' The River With

J. FRANK DOBIE—CHANGED MAN

J. Frank Dobie, at 75, admitted he'd changed with the years. The famed writer-folklorist recalled that when he was nearly 60, his mother remarked: "Son, you're getting to be like an old man." "I was interested only in the pageant of the past," said Dobie, "not in the problems of the world."

The white-haired Dobie afterward readjusted his sights, and to some extent, his company. Great old friends like writer-naturalist Roy Bedichek and historian Walter Prescott Webb were gone. Dobie was seriously ill several times.

Dobie dated his change of interest from the past to contemporary affairs about the time of World War II.

"Now I seek out the company of young men, like yourself," he courteously told this reporter, a grandfather.

"I'm never bored. It's a blessing for a human being to enjoy his own mind. I like my own company and I like the company of others."

Dobie was delighted at the company he found on the list to receive the Presidential Medal of Freedom in 1964, and particularly to be grouped with his old friend, poet-biographer Carl Sandburg.

"I've known him a third of a century," said Dobie, recalling the pleasures of drinking beer and talking with Sandburg. Also present were now-departed friends from the University of Texas, where Dobie taught for more than 30 years before severing connections in 1947 in a dispute with the board of regents.

The University of Texas, whose campus has expanded to within rock-throwing distance of Dobie's front yard on Waller Creek, remained one of his loves. A Dobie Room has been established at the new undergraduate library center, and houses his library and mementoes of a distinguished career.

While Dobie acknowledged that many changes had come over him philosophically and otherwise, some opinions hadn't changed.

For example, he never developed any affection for the 27-story University Main Building tower, which stands as a landmark for the city.

When the skyscraper was being built, Dobie told his class in Life and Literature of the Southwest: "They ought to lay that tower down and build a gallery along it, for shade. It would be better for this country and a university which has so much land."

This off-hand remark, picked up by a reporter for the *Daily Texan*, received national publicity. Dobie never made any issue of the tower's architecture, and was surprised at the attention his comment received.

"I had more affection for old 'B' hall, where I had my last office," continued Dobie, speaking of a one-time low-budget dormitory for men. It was torn down more than a quarter-century before to make way for the new Main Building and tower.

"I don't really have any opposition to the tower," Dobie continued. "It's just that concrete's more common than grass on the campus now. I belong to grass and ground."

Despite its irritations, "the world grows better all the time," in Dobie's opinion.

"I think we're getting better," he said. "I'm an evolutionist. Evolution doesn't go backward. Those who say people descended from paradise seem to think we're getting farther away from perfection all the time."

Dobie believed that culture is improving in the Southwest and the U.S.

"More people have cultivated minds," he said. "More are

aware of political, economic, social, and educational affairs than when Jim Ferguson was governor (1915-1917),'' when Dobie was a young English teacher at the University.

Dobie added with a chuckle that, although learning is more commonplace today, ''I don't know that a bigger majority is right.''

The former professor, who grew up on a South Texas ranch, loved outdoor life. He resisted some of civilization's inventions. Despite August heat, the shirt-sleeved Dobie worked on a cluttered upstairs desk, without benefit of air conditioning. Likewise, he had little use for television.

''—Takes too much time,'' he observed.

Dobie read some, but he avoided the ''slick magazines . . . too slanted.''

The author of numerous best sellers, newspaper columns, magazine articles, and pamphlets, Dobie wrote after 1910, when he started as a $12-a-week nightside reporter on the *San Antonio Express,* after his graduation from Southwestern University at Georgetown.

''I'm still learning how to write,'' he once said. ''After a million words, writing still isn't easy.''

Dobie never read one of his books after correcting the galley proofs. He moved on to another subject.

The white frame home where the Dobies lived after 1926 had a lawn which sloped to Waller Creek. His shaded back yard overlooked a park filled with pecan trees, picnickers, and playing children. Traffic streamed past the house on once-quiet Park Place, mostly students of the University Law School. Mrs. Dobie, one of the city's best gardeners, grew beautiful flowers as long as she lived.

Dobie was born Sept. 28, 1888, on a brushy ranch in Live Oak County, the background for much of his writing. After graduation from Southwestern he received a Master's degree at Columbia University; taught at the University of Texas; and served as an Army officer in World War I.

After the war, he returned to South Texas for ranching with an uncle, but soon gave it up for writing and an academic life.

His first major book, *Vaquero of the Brush Country,* was published in 1929.

Dobie took leave from the University during the 1940s, when he taught one year at Cambridge in England and another at a military school near London.

His difficulties with University regents reached a peak during the Homer P. Rainey controversy. Rainey, erstwhile University president, lost a race for governor in 1946. Dobie supported Rainey. Once Texas liberals tried to get Dobie to run for governor but he turned them down.

Mainly, Dobie was interested in life — people, horses, cattle, coyotes, growing things. Once he told this reporter that the "western" remains popular as entertainment because it gives people a sense of freedom and excitement lacking in their normal lives.

"We live in a very exciting age, but our excitement makes us uneasy about the future; it rips into our nerves like meat saws," he said. "The excitement of the Old West calls for no personal responsibility (to its readers and watchers). It is kind of soothing. We believe in free enterprise, but all modern talk about it is propaganda.

"Everybody with any sense knows that we live in a managed economy — giant government managing one side and giant business the other. The Old West is a dream of free men, free horses, free cattle, free Indians, free grass, free buffalo. It is a dream of freedom from management and, above all, of freedom from machinery . . . "

This writer and his family lived for more than 20 years just across Eastwood Park from the Dobies. The University and its tower have a special meaning for all Austin residents, and especially those who live in its shadow. Citizens here, particularly on the hills in West Austin, pay extra for lots where they can build homes with picture windows viewing the stately tower.

To football fans, the tower is best known for its orange lights. These are turned on above the top ledge to signal athletic victories. A tie score brings orange lights on two sides, white on the other two sides. Extra-significant occasions, such as winning a championship, bring bright orange lights the whole length of the tower, a spectacular sight on a black night.

When the Longhorns won a national football championship in 1963 the tower was lighted orange, top to bottom, with lights inside showing a many-storied figure ''1'' on each side.

Photos of this recognition of ''Texas No. 1'' — like Frank Dobie's remark — drew national attention.

It is said that the campus' building program was first laid out by a committee of three faculty members, none of whom drove cars.

The ''green grass, with shade'' which Dobie wanted for the university campus is giving way grudgingly to more high-rise buildings of concrete, stone, and steel. Parking space becomes an increasingly frantic problem. Frank Dobie realized that he was out of step with the times when he made his remark years ago. But a few old-timers recalled it when the University's greatest tragedy struck down from the tower.

J. EVETTS HALEY'S SENTIMENTAL VISIT

J. Evetts Haley, a rugged individual Texan in the best tradition, paid a sentimental return visit to Austin after many years. The occasion was to address Friends of the Austin Library, and the crowd overflowed the small auditorium of a branch library.

Arrow straight in his 70s Haley was firm of handshake and full of anecdote. He laughed easily and often but made no secret that he remained disgusted with big-spending, bureaucratic government which he has fought energetically for more than 40 years — usually without much success.

Haley's speech — detailed without notes — concerned a famous libel suit filed against him and the John V. Farwell family of Chicago, owners of the vast XIT Ranch in the Texas Panhandle, which the state traded for funds to build the state capitol. The book written in 1929 was titled *The XIT Ranch and the Early Days of the Llano Estacado.*

He said this early experience in history book writing warned, ''Don't tell the truth. Somebody will sue you.'' Haley's problem, and the Farwells', was that the book called several early transient residents of the Texas Panhandle "outlaws." The historian-author said there was no doubt this description fit, but the misdeeds occurred 50 years before and their descendants hired a lawyer and sued for $2,050,080.

In the foremost of the nine libel lawsuits, the plaintiffs got nothing, but the defendants settled the others for a total of $17,500 rather than spend more money in litigation. Haley reported the defense already had cost $110,000, took 14 months to prepare, and five weeks of trial.

Haley threaded his remarks with compliments for James D. Hamlin, lawyer for the ranch, about whom Haley later wrote *The Flamboyant Judge.*

Basically Haley is an historian and a cowman, and a top hand at both. But his life has been full of other activity, from helping build historical museums at Canyon — his home — and Midland, where he grew up, to a statewide race for governor in 1956. He ran fourth to Price Daniel, Ralph Yarborough, and W. Lee O'Daniel.

Haley's disputes with the federal government, and Lyndon B. Johnson, are political history. He disliked Franklin D. Roosevelt and the New Deal of 1933 so much that he took leave of the University of Texas-Austin history faculty in 1936 to campaign against FDR's re-election.

The young teacher was then "fired by inaction" from the faculty, as he puts it, despite defense by some liberals on the campus with whom he never identified politically. Haley campaigned in 1936 as a Jeffersonian Democrat.

Later he went to court—unsuccessfully—to fight a $506.11 fine imposed by the federal government against Haley and his son, Evetts Jr., for growing wheat on their own land which was fed to their own cattle. The federals charged him with exceeding the acreage allotment. Haley hates government "programs" and believes a man should be allowed to stand on his own feet.

The West Texan's greatest notice came in 1964 when he wrote the highly-critical *A Texan Looks at Lyndon: A Study in Illegitimate Power.* More than 6 million copies were circulated in 1964 when LBJ defeated Republican Barry Goldwater for the presidency. Even *A Texan Looks at Lyndon* is becoming a rare book, according to a new catalog of Haley's writings published by Betty Smedley, Austin bookseller and widow of the late Associate Justice Graham B. Smedley of the Texas Supreme Court. The Smedleys were friends of Haley in West Texas.

Haley has been urged to update *A Texan Looks at Lyndon* through the remainder of LBJ's career. But Haley apparently has decided against it.

In all, Haley has written 21 books, numerous magazine articles, and pamphlets. He is the best writer ever about pioneering of the West Texas and New Mexico plains. We are re-reading his *Charles Goodnight, Cowman and Plainsman,* which the late J. Frank Dobie called ''the greatest biography of a cattleman ever written.'' And Dobie disagreed completely with Haley on political and most philosophical matters.

Haley wrote of real men, who lived hard and dangerously. Some were good men and some were bad. Haley belongs to a rare group of Americans who grew up on a frontier and had the ability to write about it superbly. He also holds strong convictions, which he is willing to fight for. This may be old-fashioned but with such rawhide and courage the West was won.

TRIBUTE TO DeWITT REDDICK

DeWitt C. Reddick left such a rich legacy to those of us privileged to be his students that the full impact of his life can never be measured.

This warm and witty man was a truly great teacher. There are some good teachers, a few excellent teachers, but DeWitt Reddick achieved a pinnacle of ability and respect that put him in a class by himself.

I knew Dr. Reddick well for most of our lives. He was my journalism professor at the University of Texas in Austin and the best I ever had or saw, before or since. We were together many, many times after I graduated, often as fellow members of the University Presbyterian Church, where he will be remembered as one of the congregation's true saints. No task for the church, large or small, was ever inconvenient for Reddick to perform, even in his final years of illness.

Never to my knowledge did Reddick ever utter an unkind word about anyone. In a profession noted for cynicism and skepticism, Reddick never doubted the innate goodness of men and women. His ideals were so high he seemed incapable of mean thought, even when it seemed justified.

Yet he kept a steady belief in principles.

"We must learn to temper First Amendment rights with the constitutional rights of others," Reddick said in accepting a First Amendment fund award from the Austin Society of Journalists, Sigma Delta Chi.

All his life, Dr. Reddick firmly supported the First Amendment which guarantees freedom of speech and press under the U.S. Constitution. But Reddick sensed the possibility of abusing those freedoms.

Due process of law, he said, "may be interfered with through excessive publicity."

The courts, lawyers, and the media have tangled increasingly over the interpretation of First Amendment rights. The U.S. Supreme Court has been moving toward restraints on "rights" of reporters and photographers after an earlier period of almost absolute freedom. Reddick believed justice should prevail for everybody, including those being publicized.

We wondered how Reddick managed to keep his serenity when things around him seemed chaotic. During the Vietnam protest era there was turmoil at times on the University campus and an outpouring of anti-establishment feeling from many students and faculty members. Reddick never got involved in it, but saw the journalism department through troubled times.

Today, conservatism seems to be the mood on the University campus. Students are said to be more serious and motivated toward careers, although some off-campus types find this hard to believe in view of the University of Texas' campus reputation from past years.

Through depression, war, prosperity, protest, and peace. Reddick took it all in stride. He never seemed to meet a man or woman he didn't like, and certainly I never heard of anyone who knew Reddick who didn't love him.

Whether his ex-student is a country editor or a famous name like Walter Cronkite, Reddick treated us all alike. He not only taught us journalism, he taught us the importance of our life roles which is expressed by different people in different ways. Every Reddick student learned something meaningful.

"Dr. Reddick taught us to signify," Bill Moyers said later. We learned the significance of what we had set out to achieve.

Newspapers large and small, including *The Dallas Morning News,* have been staffed over the years with many Reddick disciples. He kept up with us all. Years after a student completed Reddick's course, the professor could greet him or her by name.

In all this, Marjorie Reddick helped make it possible. Dr. Reddick's wife was his helpmate in the finest sense, especially in his latter years of illness. Without her, Reddick couldn't have accomplished nearly as much as he did during a life that will continue to flourish through students and associates.

THROUGH THE EYES OF A GRANDCHILD

Letter to a granddaughter on her birthday:

Dear Laura,

When your mother was in high school we visited a neighbor, J. Frank Dobie, to get autographs on some books he had written.

"How old are you, young lady?" asked kindly, white-haired Mr. Dobie.

"Sixteen."

"Sixteen! Why that's a terrible age!" he exclaimed with a big smile.

Our friend on Waller Creek knew about teenagers. Sixteen is a difficult age — between childhood and grownup. Even at 14, one leans in both directions, which isn't easy.

You have the prospect of living many more years, and great things are in store for the years ahead. Your life already has been very interesting, since that Sept. 27 when you were born in Stuttgart, Germany, while your father served in the Army.

Your grandmother cried when he phoned from across the Atlantic to tell us about a new granddaughter. It is your grandmother's birthday too, a very special day for all of us.

How thankful you can be for a loving family — a great-grandmother with an outlook still as fresh as tomorrow; grandparents, parents, brother, and many cousins, aunts, and uncles. Families mean more the older one grows.

You also have good friends in school, in church, wherever you go. While you moved around with the Army, it was hard to keep up with your friends. Now that you live on the ranch near Lampasas, you have roots for the future.

Some city folks who never lived in the country think farm and ranch people are dumb hicks but it just shows their own ignorance. You have about everything a teen-ager enjoys in the city and much more. Lampasas schools may not have as fancy buildings as some places but you will still get a good education there.

You already have the beginnings of a fine education. We can thank Mrs. William Livar of Austin in large part for that. She taught you to read well in kindergarten, and to love reading. You couldn't fail to become educated, reading so much. Too few people ever learn to read well or to enjoy reading.

There's so much you've learned outside school, Laura. You have crossed oceans and lived in several states.

Living on the land gives a freedom enjoyed by too few of us. You can ride Spice and Lady, your horses, and care for them. You raise white doves and rabbits. Right now, two of your white doves are cooing in our back yard.

Your father says you and Spice (your favorite) deserve each other, always doing things differently. Then your cat, Columbus, won a blue ribbon in Lampasas' Spring Ho festival. Really, I think you like Christopher, the other cat, more. He prowls the pastures and sometimes brings home a live mouse as a gift.

You have learned to cook. Imagine winning $20 for first prize on your lemon cookies and then selling the cookies for $25 to help your club!

Also, you've had bumps. None was much harder than the Sunday afternoon your saddle and you came flying off Spice running fast. And having your teeth wired up for two years certainly is no fun. Now your teeth are beautiful.

Being Laura's grandfather is best of all — fishing, talking, playing dominoes, and even poker (for matches). I'm not sure your parents approved of me teaching you to play poker.

A wise man once said life is best seen through the eyes of a child. Even better is seeing it through the eyes of a grandchild.

Much love,
Granddad

WICK WOULD HAVE LOVED HIS PARTY

Wick would have loved the party held in his honor at the Headliners' Club.

On the day of a man's funeral, perhaps mourning only would be in order, under ordinary circumstances.

But there was laughter in Wick Fowler's memory, even during the funeral services as anecdotes were told about this extraordinary character who died at the age of 63. Few persons ever lived so much as Wick, regardless of their years on earth.

Hundreds considered themselves to be Fowler's best friend, for he was that kind of a fellow who did thoughtful things for individuals.

Fowler's children arranged the Headliner affair — as they said Wick wanted it. The club was then located on the 24th floor of the Westgate Building, across the street from Texas' capitol.

Every Friday for many years, there has been a meeting of newspaper, television, and political types in the Headliner Club bar — known as the Old Fitz Club, because bartender Wilbert Winn concocts what is considered to be the world's finest Old Fashioned drink using a beverage known as Old Fitzgerald.

Fowler wasn't an Old Fashioned customer. His was Whiskey Sour or Margarita, reflecting Wick's preference for the tangy things. Many a time, like a year-around Santa Claus, the rotund Fowler toured the club distributing free chili mix.

Friends wonder how Caliente Chili Co. ever managed to show a profit, what with Wick giving so much 2-alarm mix away.

Another Fowler favorite was jalapeño cheese, a fiery morsel that must be followed quickly by a cool liquid. Wick brought the cheese to the club usually in a brown bag, with a box of crackers and a butcher knife, to pass slices among the guests.

Fowler never met a stranger — and that was the way with the Friday meeting at the Headliners' Club. People from all over, mostly old-timers of the newspaper world, gathered for conversation about their departed friend.

It wasn't really a sad occasion, although there were often misty eyes. Rather, it was a time of fond recollection on the meaning of friendship in happy times and sadness.

Our own path and Wick's crossed many times. The first came in 1936 when he was a highway patrolman escorting then-Gov. James V. Allred to a centennial celebration at old Washington-on-the-Brazos. We wound up sharing a room in a Brenham hotel, with this then-cub reporter scared all night by the fact that Fowler had parked his loaded pistol on the night stand between us.

Our last meeting came just before his death, when Fowler — a physically-shattered man — caught us at an intersection of Congress Avenue and offered a ride in his car to the capitol. Everything Wick did was friendly, and he was constantly giving away. He gave us a record of his talk to the 36th Division on that last ride.

In Vietnam, Wick looked up our son-in-law at Pleiku and spent two weeks with him in a combat area, bringing home first-hand reports on our relative and gifting him with a large package of chili mix. That was Fowler.

There are so many personal stories about Fowler that the Friday's meeting in his memory barely scratched the surface in recalling those usually-happy occasions.

Which made more appropriate the poem from Alfred Lord Tennyson which former Gov. Allan Shivers recited in his eulogy to Wick at the funeral:

"Let there be no moaning at the bar when I put out to sea . . ."

When Ben Ramsey came to the state capitol in 1931 as a brand-new state representative just out of the University of Texas Law School, state government was a rather small and personal affair.

When he retired December 31, 1976, as a chairman-member of the Texas Railroad Commission, after nearly 15 years there, the sage wit of San Augustine left a government that had grown and was much more expensive than he found it.

But Ramsey never lost the personal touch, nor the conviction that a lot of the growth of government is unnecessary, if not actually wrong.

Ramsey isn't like the East Texan who said, "I've been here eighty years. I've seen a lot of changes — and been against all of them."

The veteran state official was reasonably progressive but never foolish. His career was marked with a wisdom and loyalty that is rare in any field, especially government.

It's just that Ramsey wasn't showy, or even political, in the usual sense. As a campaigner, it is said, Ramsey never ventured from his hotel in one town. Asked why he wasn't out shaking hands, Ramsey replied: "None of them is going to vote for me anyway."

But Texans did vote for Ramsey. Folks in his beloved San Augustine country twice elected him state representative. After six years out to practice law, he was elected twice as state senator. In 1949, Gov. Beauford H. Jester appointed Ramsey secretary of state, and the next year he won election as lieutenant governor over a formidable field in the Democratic primary.

Five elections later, Ramsey was still lieutenant governor — longer than any person in history — and a living legend in Texas politics for the droll and skillful manner in which he presided over the Senate.

A young reporter asked Ramsey, "When does the Senate come to order?" Without blinking, Ramsey replied: "Young man, the Senate of the State of Texas never comes to order. It just meets."

As a presiding officer, Ramsey cooled senatorial tempers with a quip, or he could be firm in getting the business accomplished in a minimum of time. Nobody ever accused Ramsey of being talkative, at least in public.

Privately, Ramsey is warm and friendly, and he is a devoted family man. Once, when his two daughters became ill while he was "stumping the state" in a campaign, Ramsey ignored his campaign schedule and returned home to stay until the daughters recovered. He also has legions of friends, mostly of long-standing, who understand and appreciate Ramsey's qualities, which strangers sometimes misinterpret as aloofness or shyness.

In 1961, after the death of Commissioner Olin Culberson, then-Gov. Price Daniel Sr. appointed Ramsey to fill the vacancy until the 1962 election. So he moved up from the handsome state salary of $4,800 then paid the lieutenant governor to $17,500 annually as railroad commissioner.

Ramsey makes no apology for his conservative political views. His private views are as conservative as his public stance. The East Texan firmly believes it is the duty of each generation to "conserve" and build on the foundations of their forefathers and without trying to change the system in one election.

In his last inaugural address as lieutenant governor in 1961, Ramsey asserted:

". . . It is not enough for us to rest upon the laurels of our forefathers. We *must* move forward. Our heritage demands a forthright policy of action today for an even greater Texas of tomorrow.

"Conditions change with passing years, but principles and processes of democratic government remain the same. Fundamentally, a good government is a responsive government . . . It is our duty to balance the budget. The deficit must be wiped out. Income must equal outgo. The cold facts of the balance sheet must be recognized."

In one of his longer addresses, lasting over five minutes, Ramsey called for "the best" schools, roads, mental hospitals, welfare, and health programs . . . "necessary services of the first class" but it never put him among the big spenders of the taxpayers' money.

Ramsey always contended there is too much spending, too much oratory, and too much waste motion in government and elsewhere.

Allen Duckworth, longtime political editor of *The Dallas Morning News,* was a friend and admirer of Ramsey although the two were quite different. Once Duckworth wrote of the lieutenant governor's dead-pan remark about a witness at a night committee session in the Senate.

"That man is working under a great handicap," a senator explained to Ramsey. "He is stone deaf — can't hear a thing."

Replied Gentle Ben: "I don't think he's handicapped. He doesn't have to listen to what he is saying."

On another occasion, a friend went to Ramsey's office-apartment in the east wing of the state capitol, and was dismayed to see about ten "Very Important People" in line, waiting to see the lieutenant governor.

The friend slipped through a side door into the apartment and was surprised to find Ramsey alone in the living room, casually reading a newspaper.

"Ben," asked the visitor, "Don't you realize there are some mighty important people waiting outside to see you?"

Without lowering his paper, Ramsey muttered: "Well, sit down and be quiet. Maybe they'll go away."

Shortly after his tough 1950 victory for lieutenant governor against eleven opponents, several of them at least as well known as he was, Ramsey tired of hearing post-mortems on why the others lost to him.

"You have overlooked one thing," he noted.

"What's that?"

"I got more votes."

Master of the one-liner, Ramsey has been called "a political paradox," the "Will Rogers of Texas politics," and some less complimentary names. The least complimentary are Texas labor leaders, who never forgave Ramsey for passing several labor regulatory bills through the Legislature while he was senator. One is the "Right-to-Work" law against compulsory union membership, which union leaders have been trying to repeal for almost thirty years without success.

He also was an advocate of regulating "loan sharks", strong law enforcement, and workable insurance regulations.

Jerry Holleman, then chief executive of the Texas Federation of Labor, who left the organization years ago, called Ramsey a "despot" lieutenant governor, but it never seemed to bother Ramsey. He directed the Senate with what cowboys call a "loose rein", letting senators have their way until they seemed to be traveling the wrong course, and then pulling them up short, often calming tempers with a quip.

His words in public as a railroad commission member have been few but meaningful.

Once when his close friend, Edward Clark, Austin attorney and former ambassador to Australia, was belaboring federal authorities in a speech at a proration hearing for messing up the oil and gas industry, Ramsey replied:

"We like to hear people's troubles," said Ramsey. "We don't know what to do either. We don't think Congress does. If they'd let (the oil and gas industry) alone, it would be highly satisfactory with this commission."

Ramsey accepted few speaking engagements. His commencement address to seniors at San Augustine High School in 1951 is as timely today as then.

Americans, especially the young, must choose between the ideological concepts of individual initiative and individual rights versus the idea that "government should be allowed to control individual activity, business activity, labor and wealth, and should have the power to dole out jobs, money, housing, and what have you as it seems fit.

"That way of thinking and the traditional American philosophy are as far apart as any two concepts can possibly be. Yet the concept of an all-powerful government has taken hold in some places in this country today to a dangerous and incredible extent . . . "

Twenty-five years later, the concept has "taken hold" more widely and to a more incredible extent.

"Are we going to continue to let the federal government grow in power and in scope until we have reached totalitarianism?" asked Ramsey.

The official said government can care adequately for the needs of its citizens, including the poor and the handicapped, with private enterprise without destroying American character or the incentive for citizens to work to better themselves.

Ramsey's affection for his beautiful home country at San Augustine permeates his conversation. While serving as acting governor in the absence of then-Gov. Allan Shivers, Ramsey once decided to ''reign'' over the state from San Augustine.

''No governor has reigned from San Augustine in a long time,'' he explained. ''I think I'll stay right here. If a fire whistle blows, I will go over to the window and look out.''

On one occasion when Ramsey was acting governor, he stayed in the lieutenant governor's office. Asked why he didn't occupy the governor's more elaborate offices, as his substitute is entitled to do, Ramsey replied:

''No use going over there. Shivers locked up everything before he went — except a chair.''

Well, why didn't Ramsey go over and sit in the governor's chair?

''This chair over here is more comfortable,'' he replied.

When Ramsey discovered that as acting governor he could draw $35 a day in that role in addition to his $10 a day as lieutenant governor, Ramsey remarked: ''That's a pretty good deal. Why doesn't Shivers go to Europe?''

With his slouch hat, loose suits, and shirt collar overhanging his coat, Ramsey sometimes resembled an unmade bed. On special occasions, such as inaugurations, his wife insisted that Ramsey get his hair cut.

''She acts like it was her hair,'' he grumbled, affectionately.

Although differing with much of the philosophy espoused by many national figures in the Democratic Party, Ramsey never wavered in his loyalty to the party which had honored him so many times.

In 1952, Gov. Allan Shivers led most of the state's top elected officials into the Republican column for Dwight D. Eisenhower, because Democratic nominee Adlai Stevenson refused to recognize Texas' claim to historic offshore boundaries of the tidelands. Ramsey didn't follow. Neither did he quarrel with his old friend Shivers. He just declined to endorse a Republican candidate—even once. The same year, Ramsey won renomination with 82.9 per cent of the Democratic vote.

As a result, Ramsey was in a unique position to help reunite Texas conservatives in the Democratic Party, and in 1955-1956 he was elected State Democratic Chairman.

Ramsey was never much of a "joiner". Besides the Democratic Party, he belonged to the Methodist Church, and state and national bar associations.

To state government, he brought patience, wit, wisdom, and talent where such qualities are all too scarce.

CARLOS ASHLEY, POET

The special quality of people of Texas' Hill Country, including politicians, is reflected in a volume of poems by Carlos Ashley, *That Spotted Sow and Other Hill Country Ballads*.

One poem entitled "Blacksnake Bill" is dedicated to the late Gov. Coke R. Stevenson, who, like Ashley, stems from pioneer days in the region. From a freight wagon driver (like Blacksnake Bill), Stevenson became governor after holding nearly every other office the state offered.

Often politicians from the Hill Country are controversial, like Lyndon B. Johnson, but they are never dull. And I don't recall any who wasn't exceptionally shrewd, often exercising greater influence than sheer numbers justify.

They are given to wise sayings, such as Ashley's "Cactus Jack" verse about the late Vice-President Garner of Uvalde:

> "We had better pay attention
> To what Cactus has to say,
> If we aim to keep our country,
> And not give it plum away."

Gov. Dolph Briscoe quotes often from his old friend, "Cactus Jack" Garner.

Even well-educated Hill Country folk speak a language all their own. Claud Gilmer of Rocksprings, for instance, speaks of futility: "It's like walking on a woodpile." Like Stevenson and Garner, Gilmer is former speaker of the Texas House of Representatives.

A former state senator, Ashley wrote verse while in Austin. For one Stevenson inauguration, he wrote "Values:"

> "Oh, the glamour and the clamor
> That attend affairs of state
> Seem to fascinate the rabble
> And impress some folks as 'great.'
> But the truth about the matter
> In the scale of loss and gain —
> Not one inauguration's worth
> A good slow 2-inch rain."

Such lines reflect the countryman's sense of importance. Ashley wrote one poem "For Politicians" concluding:

> "The urge to be smart-alec
> Is a hazardous pursuit —
> And our windy interjections
> Bear as flatulent a fruit.
> So I think a little padlock
> Might conserve a lot of breath
> Of word-eating politicians —
> Who most always choke to death."

Carlos Ashley writes ballads about the people and places he knows. His poems give a measure of immortality to Bob Sears' chili joint.

> "I've eaten Antoine's crepe suzettes," rhymes Ashley,
> A joy beyond compare;
> I've dined at old Delmonico's,
> Where famed gourmets repair;
> But no chef has ever challenged
> The high gastronomic point
> That mine was in early childhood
> In Bob Sears' chili joint."

One day, Carlos Ashley sent President Johnson a poem which he wrote, entitled "When the World Gets Out of Focus."

When the world gets out of focus
And it's foggy on the ground —
when the doubts and disillusions
keep kicking me around —
When I can't find nothin' funny
In this great land of the free,
And I get so blamed contrary
That the dogs won't bark at me —

I just saddle up Ole Baldy
And ride out across the hills —
soothing sights and sounds of nature
all my empty being fills —
Complications disentangle
And I shed the furrowed frown —
Then with heart and mind unburdened
I ride, whistling, back to town.''

Carlos Ashley has been practicing law, politics, ranching, and philosophy at San Saba and Llano for most of his life. His path crossed Lyndon Johnson's many times.

Like many others in the Hill Country, Ashley agreed with Mr. Johnson at times and disagreed with him on other occasions.

One quality of the granite and limestone hills, a hard-bitten land, is that it breeds strong men, who often disagree strongly. Coke Stevenson, the other candidate in the stormiest political campaign of Lyndon Johnson's career, also hails from the Hill Country.

When Stevenson — who ranched at Telegraph, Kimble County — was serving as governor, lieutenant governor, and speaker of the house, he often drove home from the state capitol to ''relax'' by chopping cedar trees, with which much of the Hill Country is infested.

As President, Lyndon Johnson likewise ''headed for the hills'' every chance that he got to relax.

The country, which seems to have lost its sense of humor, needs another Will Rogers.

"You can judge a man's greatness by how much he will be missed," Rogers once said.

By that measure, Will Rogers was a great American.

He joked with wisdom about public leaders and institutions, and always without meanness.

"I joked about every prominent man in my lifetime, but I never met one I didn't like" is the epitaph Rogers wrote that appears now on his memorial at Claremore, Oklahoma.

Today, you can hardly joke about anyone or anything without offending some special interest group. The women's libbers, for example, probably would edit the epitaph to read "person" instead of "man".

Much of Rogers' satire was directed at Congress. He could have a field day with the current one.

"Lord, the money we spend on government," said Rogers a half century ago. "It's not one bit better than the government we got for one-third the money 20 years ago."

How many taxpayers believe government is better than it was 20 years ago, now at triple the cost?

Another time Rogers said: "We will never get anywhere with our finances till we pass a law saying that every time we appropriate something, we got to pass another bill along with it stating where the money will come from."

In 1945, Texas voters placed in the state constitution just such a provision — the pay-as-you-go system that is unique among governments.

As a student reporter for the *Plainview Herald,* I once met the famed Rogers who was cracking jokes and drinking coffee at the local Hilton Hotel. I was too dumbstruck to remember a word the great man said.

In his youth, Rogers worked as a cowboy in West Texas and New Mexico. Here he practiced the rope tricks that later took him into rodeo and show business, where he earned the nickname "Poet Lariat" with his roping and patter.

While driving through Santa Rosa, N.M., on Interstate 40 with our 19-year-old grandson, I noticed a motor court named for Will Rogers.

I was surprised to learn my young companion had barely heard of Rogers. Then I remembered that Rogers died 45 years earlier Aug. 15, 1935, in a plane crash with Wiley Post near Point Barrow, Alaska. Rogers loved flying as he did people and horses.

All over America, citizens mourned the loss. When the news of Rogers' death came, I was riding home from a fishing trip through New Mexico with my father. It was a tragic and memorable day.

Were he alive, Rogers might like Ronald Reagan's political one-liners such as the recent crack in San Antonio: "I believe that Carter is doing his best as president. That's the problem."

For Rogers, this wit might have been too personal. Also, he preferred Democrats. This likely was because Rogers spoke for the "outsider" citizen, and for most of his life the Republicans governed the country.

Twice Rogers' name was placed in nomination for president at Democratic conventions, but any political office would have ruined Rogers' style.

The humorist-philosopher added respectability to entertainment, particularly the movies. None of his motion pictures would ever have needed a "restricted" or "parental guidance" label. Rogers was a devoted family man with three children.

The year of the 100th anniversary of Rogers' birth, a *Parade* magazine article by Bonnie Speer carried some of Rogers' memorable quotations. They included: "(We are) the only nation that ever went to potter's field in an automobile."

"Been millions made in wheat last week, but not by anybody who ever raised any."

"People don't mind spending their money if they know it isn't going for taxes."

"I don't care how little your nation is, you got a right to run it like you want to. When the big nations quit meddling, then the world will have peace."

"I can tell you what the farmer needs. He needs a punch in the jaw if he believes that either of the parties cares a damn about him after the election."

"You can get a road to anywhere out of the government, but you can't get a sandwich."

"We are a funny people. We elect our presidents, be they Republican or Democrat, then go home and dare 'em to make good."

"People are taking their comedians seriously and their politicians as a joke, when it used to be vice versa."

A TRIBUTE TO ALBERTA

The passing of Alberta Walker removed something fine and memorable from our lives.

Perhaps the first publicity Alberta ever received was a funeral notice. She had six children (two deceased), 13 grandchildren, 40 great-grandchildren, and she knew not how many other relatives.

Alberta was black, born on a Bastrop County farm which still belongs to the Walker family. She was strong in every way—character, spirit, respect for others, and in body. She lived to be almost 90, and she came into our home and lived after retiring at 65 from the University of Texas food staff.

From a background usually equated with poverty and deprivation, Alberta let none of this interfere with a positive outlook on life. Thankfully, she treated us as equals.

She admonished the womenfolk when she thought their skirts were too short, even stylishly short. When a Boston student, who became a civil rights marcher in the South, visited our son, Alberta ordered the visitor out of the kitchen when he insisted on washing his own socks.

"I does the washing here," Alberta proclaimed proudly, pointing the startled youth to the door.

Helen Corbitt, later a noted Neiman-Marcus food expert, didn't learn all her cooking from Alberta, although the two worked together at the University of Texas Tea House, then Austin's best dining place. Alberta was a splendid cook and created memorable salads.

Her macaroni and cheese became famous in our family, and she taught our grandson the unwritten recipe before he left for college.

Reared when Negroes long were denied the right to vote, Alberta refused to vote later.

"I don't know enough about these people," she explained with finality.

With compassion for all, Alberta had contempt for persons who cheated to obtain welfare, the lazy, thieves, and those who live off the efforts of others. In recent years, she lived in fear in her small cottage she owned for more than half a century on Austin's East 12th Street. While some blacks complained about the police, Alberta wished for more of them in her neighborhood.

During the 1930s, Alberta's husband went to Dallas where he found a job. To support their six children, Alberta walked more than two miles to rooming houses at the University of Texas, where she collected laundry to be delivered back later in the week, also on foot.

Despite a lifetime of low income, Alberta always seemed to have some money or could get it from a friend. She had worked for nearly everyone in our neighborhood and the corner grocery-man's father had employed Alberta and her husband long ago on a farm. Alberta was the only customer with credit at that cash grocery store.

Usually by telephone, she kept close contact with many friends and relatives. Occasionally, when being driven home, she asked to be let out at the hospital. Once she said she was visiting a nephew who had been sickly most of his life.

"He had polio when it first came out," Alberta explained.

Two white couples and about 200 blacks attended Alberta's funeral at the Mt. Zion Baptist Church here. It was an impressive service of words and music. The Rev. G. V. Clark praised the Lord for leaving Alberta Walker so long on earth to spread her love and high principles. He admonished the congregation to do likewise, and to live each day as if it were the last.

Later, this remarkable woman went to rest among her relatives in Bastrop County's St. Paul Cemetery, an unforgettable soul born in another era.

TELEGRAPHERS, A BREED APART

The death of A. S. (Hop) Hopkins, Sr. in Austin recalled the character of the rapidly-disappearing telegrapher from the American scene. The telegraph, and the colorful men who operated it, made history, particularly of the newspapers and railroads. More sophisticated communications systems have about replaced the telegraph, but none will ever erase the memories of these independent souls. Often telegraphers were rootless people, whose skill found them jobs wherever the railroads ran. Most were unusually independent, and generous. The telegraph was on its way out of newspaper communications when I entered as a young reporter. Hop Hopkins, a strong and gentle man, became a helpful friend. Surely all telegraphers were young once, but I don't remember any who didn't seem middle-aged or older. Many changed into teletype work, as Hop did. Some never even tried to adapt to the new machines.

Telegraphers used the dash-dot Morse Code, named for Samuel F. B. Morse, who invented the telegraph. A shorthand Phillips Code was used by some operators, and experts could follow either Morse or Phillips. Every telegraph instrument I ever saw (called ''bug'') had an empty tin Prince Albert tobacco can inserted in its sounding device for amplification. Why the manufacturers didn't just build the sets around a tobacco can I never knew.

A shorthand that transferred over to teletyped messages and newspaper reporting was invented by the telegraph operators. Instead of spelling out each letter for ''President of the United States'' for example, they transmitted ''POTUS''. The United States Supreme Court became ''SCOTUS'' on the telegraph.

A greeting was ''73'' and ''30'' meant the end, a number inscribed on some newsmen's tombstones.

Legislature was shortened to ''XGR'' on the wires.

A one-time boxer, Hopkins became sports editor for the *Austin American* while serving as a telegrapher at the capitol for the Associated Press.

At the University of Texas Memorial Stadium, where

reports went over leased telegraph wires to newspapers, Hop had a great advantage over fellow reporters. In the days before sports information specialists working for the schools furnished transcripts of the game's progress, Hop's telegrapher-ear caught what every one of his competitors sent over the telegraph.

He could write a sort of consensus account of a football game.

The Dallas Morning News used relays of shorthand reporters and telegraphers to transmit the complete text of a major debate between James Stephen Hogg and George W. Clark in their 1892 race for governor, a tremendous feat.

Telegraphers often were temperamental and sometimes hard drinkers. One operator serving the *Dallas News* Austin Bureau disliked sending long scholarly articles by a former editor who had moved to Austin. The writer wrote poorly on the typewriter and corrected it copiously in almost illegible longhand.

Once, the telegrapher skipped one whole page in the writer's article. It appeared in print the next day with nobody ever noticing the difference.

One Dallas telegrapher serving news wires had an aversion to high society, and detested sending stories about such social activity. It is said this man, who shall be called A. B. Jones (not his real name) habitually included his own name to the list of dignitaries and beautiful people attending these many-splendored events.

Not even the host ever had the privilege of meeting "A. B. Jones," who was listed in newspapers among important guests at the party.

HARLEY SADLER, TENT SHOWMAN

It's a pity Harley Sadler isn't around to run the tent show proposed to the U.S. Department of Agriculture to explain the food problem to the citizenry.

An assistant to former Secretary Earl L. Butz proposed the traveling show to offset what is called "a distorted picture" consumers are getting about food prices. After all, consumers are virtually being priced out of the market on many items, and

many producers — particularly livestock and milk producers —
are verging on bankruptcy. (In Dallas, Butz said he had vetoed
the show idea.)

Sadler could expose the irony in this situation and probably
inject some common sense into it.

For younger readers, Harley Sadler was a West Texan rated
the greatest tent showman in the United States. His theatrical
troupe toured the farm belt and small cities from Galveston to
Amarillo for 22 years before World War II, following the harvest
where the money was.

Harley's show mixed comedy and melodrama, with candy
salesmen roaming the aisles between acts. It had 60 people, its
own railroad cars, and a 20-piece orchestra. Smalltown West
Texans hadn't seen the likes before or since. His performers included Jennifer Jones, Chill Wills, and others who attained
movie fame.

A half-century ago, Sadler told audiences about going to
Dallas as a boy. They stayed at a small hotel, in a room with a
big white bathtub, fluffy towels, and scented soap.

"Me and Paw just stood there looking at it all, wishing it
was Saturday night," Harley recalled.

Buying a circus really put Harley out of show business, as
he discovered that elephants as well as horses ate more than people eat. Next he went into oil drilling and politics — made and
lost a fortune.

Harley beame a state representative and senator, once being defeated because he recommended a tax on bottled drinks.
He was a good legislator, but too gentle to make a big hit in the
hard world of politics. And he stayed broke giving money to
old-time show people who dropped by his Capitol office looking
for a loan. Harley never turned one down.

"I've drilled 18 dry holes and owe everybody in Abilene
except the depot," Sadler grinned.

This grim news was delivered with the wide smile of a
Toby, a red-wigged comedy character Sadler made famous in
the wheat-and-cotton country. Toby was a bumpkin type who
was continually being city-slicked by somebody but wound up
outsmarting the smarties in the last act.

"Intelligence is what enables some people to get along without an education," Sadler once said.

His humor, like Will Rogers', was always clean, and usually country.

Example: A snakebit cowboy filling out an insurance application was stumped about the question as to whether he required treatment from an accident.

"That ain't no accident," he said, "They did it on purpose."

Sadler was a devout Baptist, and — unlike most traveling shows — his was always welcome into a community.

"America is money mad," Harley once said. "We need to get off the gold standard and onto the soul standard. God alone can save our country."

This was said, of course, before America got off the gold standard, and onto whatever standard it now has.

Harley would be horrified at much of what now passes for entertainment.

The Theatre Arts Department at Texas Tech University, in a city where Sadler performed and loved, recreated a Sadler tent show.

The country could surely use a Harley Sadler to put things in perspective. Whether or not city-reared citizens would appreciate his style, Harley could talk to the lady who gathers the eggs and the fellow who milks the cow.

As he spoke to Old Brindy, an ornery cow:

"You old pot-bellied son-of-a-gun. You can drink more water and give less milk and mess up more ax handles than any cow I ever saw."

He could have been talking about some of our leaders.

JAY VESSELS AND GOOD HUNTING

The biggest complaint that Jay Vessels made about what he termed his "ticker trouble" was that it came just before the goose and duck season was opening.

The shooting started three days later down on the Lissie Prairie near Eagle Lake, where our old friend Vessels and I had watched the great flights for many years in company with Tom Waddell, one of America's great outdoorsmen, and a former game warden in the area.

Jay's "ticker" gave out following open heart surgery to repair an ailing valve, a calculated risk which he knew might likely be fatal. But our friend lived more than his threescore and ten years, fully and as unselfishly as anybody we ever knew.

The great ringnecks and snow geese over the rice fields will miss Vessels this fall, and so will Roger, a magnificent Golden Retriever belonging to Waddell. Roger hunted with us for several years, an intelligent and high disciplined dog.

Vessels wasn't a "meat hunter" but a sportsman, who enjoyed the sight, the sound, and the aroma of the outdoors even more than the sport. He took as many shots with a camera as with a gun.

The whooping cranes will never know that Jay Vessels was the best friend they ever had. While employed by the state department publicizing conservation and wildlife Vessels became the leading spokesman for saving the whooping cranes that winter in the Aransas refuge near Rockport.

Vessels annually charted the flights of the great birds from Canada to the Texas coast, where they have become a major tourist attraction, drawing hordes of birdwatchers.

Service in two wars seemed to increase Vessels' compassion for his fellow man. As an Air Force press officer in World War II, Col. Vessels established an international reputation for operating the best supplied news camp in Western Europe. As a forager, he had special talents serving war-weary newsmen on linen tableclothes with vintage wines found somewhere in the battle zone, for example.

When Vessels came to Austin to visit his old war correspondent friend, Wick Fowler, who covered World War II for *The Dallas News,* the former Minnesotan chose to stay in Texas.

His kindnesses here to friends, especially among the press, are too numerous to mention, and Vessels likely would brush aside the compliment with an epithet anyway.

Many of us will remember Jay whenever the majestic geese fly. They are part of a magnificent tradition of man and nature that belong together.

MUCH ODE TO DON GILLIS

Don Gillis was a short-haired musician in a long-haired profession. His serious talents were mixed with equal parts of humor.

When Granville Walker phoned from Fort Worth to report our old friend Gillis was dead, a flood of warm memories followed.

"If I ever start acting like people think a musician should act, stop me," Gillis once said. If temperament ever marked his great ability, we never noticed it.

After Walker's call, we replayed Gillis' record "Symphony of a Prairie School" dedicated to his alma mater, Texas Christian University. We reread parts of Gillis' serio-comic textbook titled "The Unfinished Symphony Conductor."

Several symphonies were among his accomplishments — one named "Symphony Five and One-Half." His works were played by great orchestras and great conductors, including Arturo Toscanini and Arthur Fiedler. Years ago, Gillis left TCU to try Chicago and New York, where he produced the Toscanini symphony programs on national network radio (before television).

As Gillis became executive vice president of the famed Interlochen, Mich., summer school for high school musicians, Gillis helped hundreds of talented youngsters. He traveled the world as guest conductor-composer.

He returned to Dallas during the 1960s to teach at Southern Methodist University and later Dallas Baptist College.

Gillis wrote a Texas-based musical, "Star Valley Junction."

We watched a trial performance when Gillis offered the show as part of the San Antonio HemisFair but it was turned down. In my opinion, it would have rivaled "Oklahoma" as entertainment.

Early, Gillis met the big names of show business when Amon G. Carter Sr. and Fort Worth sponsored Casa Mañana (the original with a curtain of water fountains) during the 1936 centennial.

It brought big names, like Billy Rose, Paul Whiteman, Joe Venuti, and Sally Rand. Gillis played with the kings of popular music.

There were poor but happy days for our newly-married circle of friends. Included were Granville Walker and J. Pat Henry, who became prominent ministers in Fort Worth and Dallas respectively, but then were theology students at TCU. A budding actor, Nelson Olmsted, later made it big as a character actor in television and the movies.

We shared "bologna banquets" and dreams of the future.

Don Gillis was part of nearly everything musical in Fort Worth.

He played in the Fat Stock Show Band and a Baptist church in addition to TCU, where his Horned Frog band enlivened an era of great football teams.

Developing a public appreciation of serious music was a Gillis goal. Once he produced Sunday afternoon concerts at the auditorium with Fort Worth's best musicians. Friends were enlisted to help.

Once Granville Walker was asked by Gillis whether prayer would bring customers to the concerts.

"Yes, but it would also help if we all called our friends on the telephone," came the reply.

When he died of a heart attack in South Carolina, Gillis was telling a joke.

His credits in the foreword of "Unfinished Symphony Conductor" were like these:

"To the team of Smith and Corona . . . for the use of their typewriter keys.

"To a certain Charley Webster of Requiem, Mass., . . . for use of the dictionary."

Right now, Don Gillis is probably up there playing his trombone.

"SENATOR DUCKWORTH"

Around the statehouse, friends called him "Senator Duckworth." And the political editor of *The Dallas News* appeared to relish the title.

Allen Duckworth often dressed like a dramatic version of an Old South senator — big hat, cigar, baggy suit and flowing tie. And he liked to strike a politician's stump-speaking pose, particularly when telling a story.

It is said that he once appeared on a panel program at an exclusive girls' school. Beforehand, some students mistook him for a real senator. Duckworth reportedly gave the girls a hair-raising interview about conditions down South, with Uncle Tom overtones.

Once he made a speech to students in a small North Texas town. Duckworth hadn't made many speeches and was frightened at the assignment. But he made it through with such success that he confided later to friends that it almost influenced him to run for office.

Duckworth held a special affection for political underdogs. He spoke kind words privately for Lyndon B. Johnson, and gave him friendly treatment in his news reports when it was popular to lowrate him in Texas.

Likewise, Duckworth was a friend of George C. Wallace, the spunky segregationist governor of Alabama. At a time when most journalists were heaping scorn and criticism on Wallace, Duckworth listened to Wallace's story.

The political editor's taste ran to colorful and witty people.

Included were Edward Clark, Austin attorney and U.S. ambassador to Australia; Kika de la Garza, congressman and ex-state representative, an amiable Latin American; and Bob Murphey, Nacogdoches lawyer, humorist, and candidate for the State Senate.

As Duckworth did, these men have a common quality of maintaining a serious purpose in a comic atmosphere.

Once this writer, among others on *The Dallas News,* engaged in a discussion with Duckworth over whether ''buffalo'' and ''bison'' were synonymous. The purists maintained that the shaggy animal was a bison. Duckworth stuck to buffalo, insisting nobody would ever refer to a ''bison nickel,'' for example.

The late Allen Duckworth will be greatly missed on the Texas political scene, and the state Capitol which he visited so often will be different without him. There is a unique, hard-to-describe communion among people in politics, even those who disagree sharply. Many here have joined in paying tribute to him.

VI

Gerbils, Politics and Hogs

THE WAYWARD LEGISLATURE

Once I received a copy of a newspaper article written from Washington reporting the Texas Legislature "recently" had passed a law giving the mathematical symbol pi a value of three rather than 3.14159.

Everyone who passes high school geometry knows pi equals 3.14159.

The trouble with the aforesaid article is that it is untrue. The man who seriously reported this matter said Texas lawmakers simply figured it would be easier to use number three than the real value of pi.

This is a silly fiction that has been kicked around about legislative bodies for a long time and it is astonishing that a newspaper reporter would repeat the canard without checking the facts.

The same article asserted erroneously that the Texas House of Representatives "a few years back erupted into a splendid fistfight in which roughly half the 150 members insulted wives and mothers, questioned mutual breeding, overturned desks and chairs, tumbled into one another and gleefully punched out deskmates and friends. In the midst of the melee, four calmer members strode to the dais and warbled "I Had a Dream Dear' in perfect barbershop harmony."

If this ever happened, nobody around here knew it. Apparently, it is just more barroom fantasy about how Texas laws are made.

There is plenty of foolishness around any legislative body, without embellishing the truth. Texas lawmakers have done such things as adopt a memorial resolution honoring the Boston

Strangler, when they were misled because nobody except the sponsors knew the man named in the resolution was the notorious murderer. It was introduced by a representative wanting to prove legislators seldom pay much attention to the resolutions they adopt, which ordinarly just praise some citizen in a politician's home district.

The alleged humor about Texas legislators amending the value of pi and representatives engaging in a free-for-all fistfight appeared in a series written for the Gannett News Service "exploring the cultural, political, social, and economic differences between the North and the South in America . . . ''

The South lost in that comparison, which isn't surprising considering what was said about Texas.

The article came to me after Dr. Arthur A. Smith, the distinguished economist for the First National Bank in Dallas (now retired), spotted it in a Springfield, Mo., newspaper.

"I could scarcely believe what I read . . . '' Dr. Smith wrote to an old friend in Springfield. "It is an example of irresponsible journalism . . . ''

Legislators have always been under public scrutiny which they should be. Some take advantage of their positions. Every one had human frailties, but collectively they operate the best system of government ever devised.

A few rant and rave in debate. I never saw or heard of one hitting another member during a legislative session. There have been threats and fist-shaking, always at a distance where the sergeant-at-arms could keep the "warriors" safely apart. Once I saw an irate senator throw an inkwell at a representative. It missed. This was the closest call to violence I ever witnessed in years inside the statehouse.

Years ago, some legislators would come back to the Capitol for night sessions after too long with the cocktail crowd. That has even happened to reporters. I have never seen anything worse than boisterous conduct, a member snoring at his desk, or somebody trying to argue about everything. During the tense days of World War II, when several members were leaving for military service, a night session produced about 20 young men who got drunker as the evening progressed, having a cache of liquor in the men's lounge. Before it was over, they were playfully tearing each other's shirts.

Shortly afterward, the session adjourned, and night sessions in the House of Representatives have been relatively scarce ever since.

LOBBYISTS ARE THE DARNDEST PEOPLE

A colleague of ours in Dallas expressed surprise that a state legislator was unable to explain a bill he had introduced. The representative was waiting on a lobbyist, who furnished him with the bill, to give him an explanation of it.

Anyone around the Legislature who would be surprised at this procedure must also believe in the stork theory. The practice of ''lobbyists'' writing bills, and also telling the sponsor what is in them, is about as old as lawmaking.

However, this isn't necessarily sinister. It depends on the integrity of the lobbyist and the judgment of the legislator after having the proposal in hand. Bills frequently are introduced in a hurry because there is a deadline at each legislative session. The explanation really becomes important later, when the measure faces committee hearings and legislative debate.

Representatives and senators once did most of their own bill writing, usually in law offices before coming to Austin. Here, too, the influence of special interests can be felt. So the public may be as well-served today as in the days when the lawmaker actually wrote the new laws, rather than having others do the actual draftsmanship.

A few bills and resolutions each session will actually be authored by a legislator. By far the largest source of legislation, however, is the Texas Legislative Council. Its staff of a dozen lawyers and several non-lawyer assistants prepares about three-fourths of the bills and resolutions introduced in the Legislature.

Each Legislature receives several thousand bills and resolutions. The bills represent attempts to change the law. Some of the resolutions seek to amend the constitution. Others would create special studies. Most resolutions are memorials to distinguished citizens who die, or recognize unusual achievement —

such as a local high school winning the football championship.

The record for the percentage of bills passed is about 30 per cent of those introduced. The mass of proposed legislation is virtually impossible for an individual to read much less for individual lawmakers to write.

Since the legislative council got involved in bill writing, the mechanics have improved greatly. Its staff works on instructions from a legislator or a state agency which has a legislator sponsor.

A major problem legislators face is accuracy of the explanations furnished to them with bills. Like ordinary mortals, lawmakers must operate largely on faith they are doing right — based often on what others tell them about the effect of their actions.

Since there is a tendency to enact the explanation rather than the actual bill, because the explanation is written in more understandable terms, lawmakers are dependent on the accuracy of what they are told. Serious problems have developed over this. Often the explanation is partisan and may conceal more than it reveals about the true purpose of a bill.

When the session adjourns, lawmakers go home just hoping they did right.

TOSS THE BULL, BUT NO BETTING

The state's 1905 law governing contest roping was overhauled by the Legislature in 1965.

Texans and visitors who watch Fourth of July rodeos and roping contests in many large and small arenas may be unaware of the longtime concern of ranchers, humane societies, and legislators — as well as contestants and the public.

The new law adds ''grown cattle'' and ''other animals'' to calves and goats as legal objects for roping in contests.

Originally, Rep. Tom Holmes of Granbury proposed in 1965 to repeal the law which once virtually outlawed the roping — in contests — of live animals by men on horseback.

Once roping contests were against the law. Local historians say this was not any proposal of the humane societies, but of cattle owners.

Cowboys who roped cattle and calves—belonging to someone else — during the open-range days were said to have damaged valuable beef by ''chousing'' the animals, throwing cows or calves on the ground, and sometimes causing injury by dragging them with horses.

So ranchers had the Legislature pass a law against this sport in which cowboys often engaged during their spare time, usually accompanied by betting.

The growth of rodeos as a spectator sport, and with prizes replacing the wager as an attraction for contestants, changed roping contests almost into a social event in some communities. Many Texas cities have lighted roping arenas, with grandstands, where roping contests are held regularly. Calves, usually those of Brahma blood because they are trickier and more durable than ordinary beef breeds, are used for most roping contests.

Roping clubs and rodeos have made catching calves and goats with lariats by men on horseback a rather sophisticated event, involving pens and chutes. In the open-range days, it doubtless was a rougher game, both on men and animals.

Anti-cruelty-to-animal groups still seek to curb some rodeo and roping club practices. The public generally is not aware of the long and sometimes bitter controversy there has been between livestock raisers and handlers, and the humane societies. Proposed humane laws often run afoul of what ranchers consider ordinary and necessary practices — such as branding animals.

The new roping law serves as a reminder that ''modern'' Texas really isn't far from the open-range day.

WASTING TIME WITH LAWYERS

It would do every lawyer good to serve on a jury. Most lawyers avoid putting other lawyers on a jury for fear they might be too persuasive in the jury room.

A juror gets the impression that the courts operate mainly for the benefit of lawyers. At least, that is the impression this juror got in a week of service in both criminal and civil cases in Travis County.

Most of the time was spent waiting — waiting for something for the jurors to do. Judges in both the criminal and civil courts repeatedly apologized for taking up the time of busy men. The panel of one hundred included bankers, business and professional men, skilled craftsmen, barbers, salesmen, and numerous government workers.

The men summoned didn't mind the jury service, but they did object to wasting time. The civil case was delayed one morning by an attorney's absence at the hospital, attending the tonsil operation of his child.

"Didn't he know yesterday that the operation would be done today?" grumbled one juror, whose own business was suffering from his absence.

"If I was a lawyer, I'd be on time —and brief," remarked another juror. "Don't lawyers realize how jurors feel about having their time taken up unnecessarily?"

Frequently, the judge disposes of divorces and criminal cases where the defendants want to plead guilty, while the whole jury panel stands by. The panel collectively wishes these time-taking matters could be handled without the presence of a jury.

There is, of course, an advantage in having the panel on duty, even though no jury is used. A lawbreaker often decides to plead guilty when he scans the roomful of men waiting to try his case. Many a civil suit is settled also on the day it is scheduled to go to trial.

The Texas Judicial Council and other groups are trying to get better juries. One way is to make men more willing to serve. Courts — and lawyers — should be more considerate of the jury's time. A lawyer who is considerate of the jury's time is more likely to get a favorable decision. It's just good jury relations.

District Judge J. Harris Gardner of Austin had an outstanding record of persuading men to serve on juries. Judge Gardner will excuse a person, but it is usually easier to take your turn on the jury panel than it is to get excused by Judge Gardner. He lets citizens select the most convenient week to be on the jury, but Judge Gardner strongly urges each man to pick a week rather than getting off entirely.

The Judicial Council believes that too many Texans are exempt from jury service. So far, the Legislature has turned a deaf ear to the plea. Perhaps the most important change urged by the council is raising the automatic exemption age from sixty to seventy. Thousands of men in their sixties are better able to serve on juries than younger men. Moreover, they have mature judgment.

The 60-year limit was imposed before the life span reached its present high level. There is little reason for keeping the restriction now.

IT'S NOT NICE TO BE DISCRIMINATING

Honors given Roy Wilkins, longtime executive director of the National Association for Advancement of Colored People, call to mind a problem of semantics in identifying ethnic origin. We aren't talking about the matter of pronouncing a word, which got comptroller Robert S. Calvert into so much trouble.

Just choosing the right word —such as what to call a black American of African descent —is our subject. Somewhat unfortunately, the meaning of words change. "Colored" once was a term of highest respect in referring to a Negro. Roy Wilkins once was quoted as saying he thinks "colored" still is "well-placed" in the name of his organization.

The National Association for Advancement of Colored People has been in the forefront of the long struggle for racial rights. It has been one of the most responsible organizations in that direction, and the Zale Corp. wisely chose director Wilkins to receive the $25,000 annual award for outstanding contribution to civil rights.

Yet "colored" is practically a "no-no" in addressing modern blacks. "I'm not colored. I'm black," is the reply a white is likely to get these days if he uses the term in describing a person of Negro ancestry.

In our quarter-century of writing about race relations, phraseology has changed greatly, not to mention pronunciation. "Negro" once was the acceptable term, but the southern pronunciation didn't fit the accent of non-southern reformers, who were also among the first to discard "colored" as a description of black citizens.

This left the NAACP in a somewhat embarrassing position,

since it could hardly change its name after having become identified as the nation's greatest leader in civil rights. The semantics circle has included "African," "Afro-American," "Afro," and other terminology before "black" came into vogue as apparently the most acceptable word presently.

Americans of other ethnic groups, particularly of Mexican origin, have undergone a similar quandary. So have Indians, once described by tribal names; later as "American Indians" to distinguish them from the citizens of India.

After two generations of effort to erase racial identity in the United States in a "common man" movement, the trend now is toward trying to identify racial background. Courts have ordered this for public school purposes. Congress has legislated it for employment purposes.

Once "American" seemed an adequate word for everybody living in the U.S. even though Texas alone has at least 22 identifiable racial groups, each with pride of ancestry and culture.

Presently the trend seems toward polarization of races, notwithstanding the best efforts in the other direction by NAACP and similar organizations, courts, Congress, legislatures, churches, schools, and various social planners.

Perhaps we are learning that ethnic families can live in the same country peaceably without having to be alike, or even liking and disliking the same music, accents, food, and football players.

Once it was in good taste to be "discriminating." Some day "discrimination" may again become a respectable word, stripped of its racial connotation.

TEXAS MISSED THE TELEGRAPH

The course of the War Between the States might have been changed had the Confederacy made better use of the telegraph.

That opinion was voiced at a meeting of the Texas State Historical Association by Charles H. Dillon, a Dallas man who has done extensive research on the history of the telegraph in the Southwest. Dillon retired from Western Union after 30 years service and now represents a national auditing firm.

"Early in the Civil War, (President) Lincoln set up a military telegraph department and personally spent a great deal of his time keeping in touch with the telegraphic dispatches from his General,'' Dillon reported.

''The Confederacy did not take this step until late in the war after many of the lines in its territory had been destroyed or seized by Federal forces.

''Had they been more alert to use the telegraph, the outcome of the Civil War could have been either different or postponed.''

The speaker said critics should go slow on this point, however, as the 1861-1865 conflict was the first in which electric communications were available. The telephone came 20 years later.

The first telegraph line was strung into Texas, from Shreveport to Marshall, in 1854 — just 40 days after the Texas Telegraph Company received its charter.

Using trees and posts for poles, the wires quickly were extended through East Texas to Henderson, Rusk, Palestine, Crockett, Montgomery, Houston, and Galveston.

The infant system had much trouble in its early years, from weather and from wagoners who often used the telegraph poles for firewood. The company got into serious financial difficulty, Dillon said, but was revived in 1859 by newspaper and railroad interests of Houston and Galveston. On Jan. 24, 1860, the first permanent telegraph wire in Texas went into operation between Houston and Galveston, crossing Galveston Bay on a railroad bridge.

The line continues in use today, while its predecessors have disappeared, Dillon said. Even occupation of Galveston by Federal troops in 1862 failed to disrupt the service, and the recapture of the island was reported later over this wire by Gen. Bankhead Magruder.

Generally, however, the war wrecked the South's telegraph system. Otherwise, Dillon said, one battle of the war might never have occurred. He referred to the Battle of Palmito Hill (Brownsville), which took place after General Lee had surrendered his army at Appomattox.

After 1865, the telegraph spread through East Texas. The

first line reached Dallas in 1871, but a financial panic stopped the extension to Fort Worth for three years.

Sixteen thousand miles of telegraph wires connected Texas cities with each other and the outside world by 1915, Dillon said, even though competition had come from the telephone.

The Republic of Texas in 1839 passed up a chance, already noted by historians, to be first in using the telegraph invented by Samuel F. B. Morse. The inventor tendered the device to then-President Mirabeau B. Lamar for "perpetual use" but never received an acceptance.

Five years later, the U.S. government built the first telegraph line from Washington to Baltimore.

Historian Dillon quoted a *San Antonio Express* editorial of March 12, 1916:

"Had the fathers of the Republic of Texas accepted the gift of Samuel F. B. Morse . . . this state today would have been the one in the union forever free of taxation. The worldwide royalties from the telegraph would not only have paid all expenses of the state government, but at the same time created a sinking fund of millions."

TO SCOTLAND, WITH LOVE, TEXAS

There's a wee mystery about how a ballad of the Texas Rangers got into auld Scotland.

Kenneth Goldstein, an anthropologist from the University of Pennsylvania, revealed to the American Folklore Society that two similar versions of a Ranger song are sung by the Scots. He recorded one sung by Lucy Stewart, 59, in Aberdeenshire last year.

Another which Goldstein played for more than 50 folklorists in the Driskill Hotel's Maximilian ballroom was recorded in 1954 by Geordie Robertson, then 82, of Aberdeen.

The ballad tells how a youth failed to heed his mother's warning against leaving home to join "a gallant band." The Robertson version said:

"We march't from Siatonia (pronounced like San Antonio) into the Royal Gran' (like Rio Grande) . . . "

Miss Robertson sang "I marched from Aberdeenshire into the Royal Gran'." She thought it referred to a mutiny in India.

Both ballads relate how the Indians beset the Rangers leaving dead and wounded all over the place.

They conclude, in what Goldstein said is a previously unrecorded verse:

''Come a' ye's gallant Rangers aroun' me here this night,
''Whatever you do for a livin', for God's sake nivir fight,
''Your enemy is quite careless, they shoot right in the crew
—they're boun' tae hit somebody an' perhaps it might be you.''

Goldstein said opinions differ on how the ballad got to Scotland. He cited it as an example of folklore which America exports. Goldstein thinks the Ranger song probably was carried back to Aberdeen by an itinerant Scot visitor to the United States. Some others think the Buffalo Bill Wild West Show left the song during a European tour in 1902-1904.

Scotsmen had a big hand in the Texas cattle industry during the last century, and may have picked up the song here. Investors from Scotland had large land and ranch holdings in Texas and frequently came here.

Americans have left folk music at many places overseas, Goldstein said. One example, he said, is ''The Streets of Laredo,'' a Texas border ballad which Scots learned from GIs during World War II.

Cowboy songs also went up the Chisholm Trail from Texas into Canada's prairie provinces, reported Mrs. Edith Fowke of Toronto, who conducts a folklore program for Canadian Broadcasting Company.

Mrs. Fowke said the Western Canadians drew most of their ballads from the American West. Most deal with the hardship of drouth and cold, and the loneliness of being far away from home.

One of the best-known ''Texas'' ballads, however, may have originated in Canada, Mrs. Fowke said.

''Red River Valley,'' which most folk consider to be a song of Texas-Oklahoma, had been thought to be based on an older New York ballad called ''Bright Mohawk Valley.''

Mrs. Fowke reported that a ''Red River Valley was sung in Canada many years ago, based on the so-called ''Red River Rebellion'' of 1869 in Manitoba. She explained that circumstances would appear to preclude the Canadians from having picked up the American version first.

Gerbil-watching comes easy to a fellow who earns his salary watching the Texas Legislature.

Once, we came into possession of a pair of these furry little animals while their young owners were engaged in moving from Alabama to Texas.

The size of the Generation Gap is revealed by the fact that until these Gerbils came into our life, we had never heard of the fascinating little creatures. But the small-fry and even young parents set are up to the ears in Gerbil lore.

The Gerbil looks like an overgrown mouse, or undersized hamster, and is much more sociable. The first ones were brought to this country a few years ago for medical research. It was learned that Gerbils make nice pets around the house.

We quickly discovered that you shouldn't squeeze the Gerbil. He will bite. But you can pick him up by the tail, or do almost anything else to the animal so long as he doesn't feel too hemmed in. Furthermore, Gerbils are goosy, hard to catch but easy to pet.

Ours are named Speedy and Frederick. They are brothers, but the similarity ends there.

This is where the analogy with observing our lawmakers commences.

Speedy, who might well be a Gerbil Senator, races around the exercise wheel in the cage at a giddy pace. He can attain high speed and even loop-the-loop inside the wire wheel. Speedy runs clockwise.

Frederick (don't ask me how they get the names) might qualify as a Gerbil Representative. He runs in the opposite direction from Speedy in the exerciser. Fred is a counter-clockwise Gerbil.

This leads to real complications when the Gerbils attempt to use the exerciser together. Speedy puts more power in his clockwise sprint. Frederick is slower on the counter-clockwise tread, but he does manage to keep Speedy from dominating their joint operation completely. Occasionally, Speedy turns Freddie a full flip in their opposite pull of Gerbil-power.

The pair burrows down together at night, except when they

decide to take a nocturnal spin on the sprint-wheel.

Speedy and Frederick do run a lot, except they just do not seem to be going anywhere.

We were discussing the Gerbils with Millard K. Neptune, a businessman. Outsiders may be surprised to learn that what appears to be a deep political discourse may be really a conversation about household pets.

The Neptunes once received from their son, away in school, a 3-foot Boa Constrictor who evidently didn't fit into campus life.

The young snake ate very seldom. His diet consisted of an occasional live mouse, eaten whole. The Neptunes kept the snake healthy on mice purchased at a pet store.

One day, while the son was at home, the pet store ran out of mice. Young Neptune bought a small rat for his pet boa, and put it in the cage.

Next morning the boa was dead and the rat still running around the cage. The snake expired from a bite on the head.

Without much show of regret, Neptune Sr. said of the boa: ''His lunch ate him.''

These parables about pets may not fit everyone's present situation, but we still think Speedy and Fred can qualify as candidates for the Gerbil Legislature after a bit more practice running around in circles.

HOT MEAL FOR HOGS?

Eager members of each new Texas Legislature should be sobered by the thought that very few major problems of state ever get solved.

New ideas in legislation and government seldom arise.

Take Gov. William P. Clements' recommendation for initiative and referendum. It is hardly new, simply an outgrowth of the old town meetings system that prevailed in the American colonies and still is practiced in some places in New England.

We like the idea even if some lobbyists and elected officials do not. It helps keep lawmakers mindful of how their actions will strike the voters. It isn't too democratic. Too many laws get passed with too little regard for the public as a whole.

All three of the state's top officials — Gov. Clements, Lt.

Gov. William Hobby, and Speaker Bill Clayton — have recommended setting aside $1 billion or so of the state's surplus revenue for the day when tax money will be harder to raise.

This thought is nearly as old as any of the three named proponents. With a few interruptions, the state's tax structure based on sales, oil and gas production — plus inflated prices — has brought a ''surplus'' for spending by every new legislature since 1940. And our representatives and senators have had little difficulty spending it all. The only thing that has stopped most sessions from spending more is the ''pay as you go'' amendment to the constitution, effective in 1945, which forbids spending beyond the estimated income of the next two years.

Scanning what we have written about the Texas Legislature over the years, one is impressed by how much money and energy goes into lawmaking with so little results. Legislators just keep chipping away at old problems, compounded by a growing population, inflation, and the change of Texas from a rural to an industrial state.

At the end of World War II, lawmakers pondered what to do about school finance, water shortages, racial desegregation, financing college construction, control over lobbying and contributions to politicians, and the hazard of building a dependence on oil imports. Sound familiar for the 1980s?

Gov. Coke Stevenson questioned in 1947 the wisdom of sending Texas natural gas to northeast industrial states to fire boilers then depending on coal for fuel. Today, government is trying to get this process reversed — from gas back to coal.

Once we thought the legislature and the voters had one problem licked. This was the financing for highway construction and maintenance.

In 1946, the voters approved a constitutional amendment directing that three-fourths of all state taxes collected from motor fuel users be allocated for keeping up the highway system. For years, increased gasoline consumption and taxes kept the money flowing for building and maintaining Texas roads in good condition.

In recent years, however, that dream faded when the decline in gasoline consumption, higher-mileage cars, and the skyrocketing cost of urban road construction caused Gov. Dolph Briscoe and the legislature to supplement ''road user'' revenues with millions from general tax sources.

In 1947, the voters approved a special ad valorem state tax for buildings on campuses excluded from the University of Texas and Texas A&M's Permanent University Fund endowment. That property tax continued for 30 years, yet one of the biggest fights in the 1981 session may be over earmarking all the PUF's income ($125 million last year) for capital improvements at selected schools or dividing it more widely.

Parenthetically, the clippings disclose that in 1958 the Coordinator of Higher Education, then Ralph T. Green, asserted Texas schools had too much money for building and too little for other purposes.

We discovered one legislative problem that apparently did go away. When Dolph Briscoe was a representative from Uvalde in the 1950s, he sponsored a bill that became labeled ''hot meals for hogs'' by its detractors. It called for cooking garbage before feeding it to swine to stop the spread of some disease. Apparently the bill died.

PIE ARE SQUARE, BUT NOT IN TEXAS

Lt. Gov. Bill Hobby has expanded our meager knowledge of applying mathematics to legislation.

Judging from the absence of mail and comment, most of you skipped our essay correcting a Washington writer's report that the Texas Legislature had passed a law to change the value of the mathematical symbol pi which the scholars calculate as 3.14159. This can be carried to many more decimal places if you want to be technical.

Texas lawmakers, our critic said, voted to change pi to the numeral three because it is easier to remember and work with.

The drawback is that three won't work when you are figuring the area of a circle. The area is radius squared times pi (3.14159).

Gov. Hobby sent us a 200-page book titled *The History of Pi* which tells us at least as much as we wish to know on the subject. It turned out to be an interesting volume in its second edition written by Peter Beckmann of the University of Colorado's electrical engineering department.

Beckmann explained he felt qualified to discuss the subject objectively since he is neither a historian nor a mathematician.

Leaping across 173 pages from history's first effort of mankind to establish the true value of pi, the book relates that a bill to set a value of pi was indeed introduced in an American legislature — Indiana's — in 1897.

Apparently the bill got no further than filing a copy in the Indiana State Archives. The measure prepared by an Indiana physician was introduced by his representative, Taylor I. Record of Posey County.

Don't ask me to explain this, but the proposed law would have declared "the circular area is to the quadrant of the circumference, as the area of an equilateral rectangle is to the square of one side." Beckmann concluded the proposal "does not make any sense at all." In that, it is hardly unique in the annals of legislation.

Beckmann said computers are virtually wearing themselves out trying to get a closer value than the Chinese and Greeks did centuries ago.

Before dropping the subject, I must repeat the story told by Mrs. Charles E. (Mary) Simons of Dallas about the uneducated country couple who sent their son off to college.

As the student got off the train on his first trip home, the youth was met by his proud parents and other kinfolk.

"Say something in algebra, son," the mother requested in front of the homecoming crowd.

"Pi R square," came the reply.

"Aw, shucks, son," said the disappointed mother. Everybody around her knows pies are round. Corn bread are square."

Research revealed that our lieutenant governor, who holds a history degree from Rice University, is a mathematics buff.

Awhile back *The Journal of Irreproducible Results,* off-beat magazine for scientists, printed Hobby's piece on mathematics of the Texas Senate, over which the lieutenant governor presides.

Hobby explained the irrationality of trying to divide 31,

the number of senators, by almost any factor. It takes two-thirds of the membership to adopt a constitutional amendment but two-thirds will not divide exactly into 31. So the rules require 21 votes, the closest you can get. Same thing applies to the four-fifths vote required to suspend constitutional rules. Obviously, as Hobby pointed out, a senator cannot be divided into fractions.

Our second highest official made whimsical observations on measuring a senator's influence. The main plus factors are years of service in the senate, importance of committee chairman-ships, and whether the senator is listed among *Texas Monthly's* "10 worst," Hobby said.

The senator's influence declines by this grading if Common Cause approves his voting record, or the member is a Republican.

TEXAS POLITICS — IN BRIEF

An assignment handed me by Fred Pass, editor of the esteemed *Texas Almanac*, recalled a story about two of my favorite old-time Capitol news reporters.

Byron C. Utecht, a dour but witty writer for the *Fort Worth Star-Telegram*, was confined to an Austin hospital.

Gordon K. Shearer, chief of the United Press (Interna-tional) bureau here, went out to see his sick friend.

Afterward Shearer wrote a brief story about Utecht being laid up.

"Asked what he was doing to pass time while in the hos-pital, Utecht replied, 'I am writing a history of the world in 1,000 words.'" To which Shearer added a postscript: "He is leaving out some details."

Pass invited me to write a political history of Texas, from the date of the almanac's first appearance in 1857. He said it could run 3,000 or 4,000 words. So I am leaving out some details.

After writing my account of politics in Texas up to 1900, I discovered I'd used up more than half my word allotment. So I also abbreviated the period I knew the most about — politics in this century.

Research emphasized points that caught my attention. On some, historians may even disagree.

Here are some points that interested me:

Sam Houston wasn't very popular with some of his contemporaries, who even questioned his conduct of the War of Independence against Mexico. He was elected governor in 1859, backed by Independents and Know Nothing Party members. A legislature loyal to the Confederacy ousted Houston in 1861 because he opposed secession. Also, Houston lost his first race for governor as a Democrat in 1857, after having been president of the republic and U.S. senator from Texas.

I hadn't realized before how strongly emotions ran over Houston's attempt to keep Texas in the United States.

Texas today has more Republicans, more blacks, and more women in state offices than ever before — at least since military government ended in the 1870s and ex-Confederates were permitted to hold office and vote again. Mexican-American representation in the legislature, based on surnames, may or may not be a recorded number.

Although Negroes served in the legislature from 1871 until 1899, none was elected between 1900 and 1967. The Democratic Party held a ''white man's primary'' in Texas after the turn of the century.

Historians assert the requirement for voters to pay a $1.75 poll tax for voting was aimed primarily at discouraging participation by tenant farmers and poor laborers in the Populist Party, which for 20 years had been challenging the Democrats' domination of Texas politics.

Two amendments to the U.S. Constitution were adopted in 1918-1919 during the administration for Gov. William P. Hobby Sr., father of the present lieutenant governor. One permitted women to vote; the other prohibited manufacture or sale of alcoholic beverages.

The year 1901 brought two rather unrelated events which shaped the state's future in a tremendous way. One was the discovery of the Spindletop oilfield in Jefferson County, Texas' first major producer. The other was the appearance of automobiles, until then experimental, on Texas roads.

One Texas governor was almost hanged before he took office. Edmund J. Davis left Texas when it joined the Confederacy in 1861 and he organized a pro-Union army in Mexico. But he was later captured, and barely escaped the noose. Federal troops, Negroes, and carpetbaggers (immigrants from the North) put Davis in the governorship in 1870.

President U.S. Grant rejected Republican Davis' claim to election in 1873 when former Confederates chose Democrat Richard Coke for the office.

THE LOST HOGG ''ADDRESS''

An historic dispute over ranchers in the Texas Panhandle fencing public land brought a controversial effort to remove a district judge by legislative ''address'' in 1887. The story is related in University of Texas historian Robert C. Cotner's biography of James Stephen Hogg.

Strong characters dominate the melodrama, a more stimulating tale than the semi-sordid case of Don Yarbrough, who resigned from the Texas Supreme Court rather than face removal by ''address.''

Jim Hogg was an ambitious East Texan who became attorney general and later governor. His chief adversary in the 1887 battle was Charles Goodnight, a famous pioneer cattleman of the northwest Texas plains and Palo Duro Canyon.

The Dallas Morning News is credited with publicizing the situation which brought the unsuccessful attempt to remove Frank Willis as judge of the sprawling Panhandle-Plains district. This newspaper sent John E. Thornton, the first ''capitol correspondent'' in Austin, to the Panhandle in 1885 to investigate the free use of state land by the ranchers. An accompanying editorial barrage contended the users should be forced to pay for grazing their livestock on land owned by the state.

Further, Goodnight and some fellow ranchers had fenced part of the state-owned prairie to keep their stock from straying and to separate them from fever-carrying South Texas cattle being driven up the trail to the Midwest.

Goodnight and the Panhandle Stockmen's Association tried to get the Legislature to pass a lease law in 1880 but the effort was killed by ''free grass'' advocates. In 1883, the Legislature prescribed a four cents per acre minimum lease on a bid basis. The ranchers bid four cents—non-competitively—for the state land they were already pasturing. A state board raised the fee to eight cents, which cattlemen said was illegal.

In 1885, Atty. Gen. John D. Templeton told the district attorney to file charges against the ranchers for illegally fencing state land. Since only 1,500 people lived in the whole 26 counties, it was virtually impossible to find disinterested grand jurors and jurors. Goodnight was foreman of a grand jury which indicted its own foreman and several other grand jurors. Eighty-six indictments were returned and 56 tried before Judge Willis and juries composed mostly of cowboys working for the defendants.

Defendants contended they had submitted legal four cent an acre payments to the land board, which refused to accept the money. Goodnight dramatized his effort by taking a wheelbarrow full of money up Congress Avenue from his hotel to the land office, offering payment at four cents an acre on 200,000 acres.

The state office's refusal to accept the money was cited as evidence supporting Goodnight at the trial. The defendants were acquitted.

Succeeding Templeton, Atty. Gen. Hogg asked the Legislature to oust Judge Willis by ''address.'' He argued the case himself before a House committee, charging conspiracy, fraud, and corruption in Willis' court. Goodnight and other ranchers lobbied in Austin for their friend, Judge Willis. The House adopted the ''address'' resolution 67 to 21, more than the required two-thirds.

Acting separately, the Senate rejected the proposal, 5 for, 22 against.

Judge Willis had argued capably in his own defense, said Dr. Cotner, describing the ''problems created in establishing normal functions of government before the population is ready to conduct them properly.''

Perhaps Judge Willis' court meted out a type of frontier justice, but Jim Hogg couldn't prove it was wrong to the Texas Senate. Goodnight won and Hogg lost. Later, Hogg became one of Texas' best-known governors. He probably didn't bother to campaign in the Panhandle area.

PAUL WHO, RODE WHAT?

We have undergone the unnerving experience of reading in a scientific journal how Henry Wadsworth Longfellow botched up the account of Paul Revere's famous ride. Since April 18 was the anniversary of the historic event, we pass along intelligence gleaned from the April 1973 issue of *Smithsonian,* the magazine published by the prestigious institution in Washington.

It tends to confirm our suspicion that writers sometimes take so much poetic license that any resemblance to the facts is purely coincidental. The most charitable thing that can be said is that Longfellow was a much better poet than historian.

In Longfellow's case, the main thing he got right was Paul Revere's name. But the rest of this familiar poem of Paul Revere's ride was taken as gospel by the teachers and students of our generation, and probably many other generations.

Richard W. O'Donnell, a Boston writer of the much-researched magazine article, expressed doubt that Paul Revere ever knew the name of his noted steed. The "steed flying fearless and fleet" was borrowed by Revere from Deacon John Larkin, Mass., who in turn had it on loan from his father.

Boston patriots paid Revere four to five shillings to make the ride, warning colonial Minute Men that the British were marching on Lexington and Concord.

Contrary to the poem, Revere didn't wait in Charlestown for the "one if by land, two if by sea" lantern signal to be flashed from the tower of Old North Church. The magazine says Paul was still in Boston when the signal came, and that confusion reigned over whether it was two if by land, or the other way 'round.

When Revere borrowed the horse for his historic ride, he didn't give his publicized "cry of alarm to every Middlesex village and farm," according to the new account. This wasn't in Longfellow's poem, but Paul, a parttime poet, did claim he "alarmed almost every house" on the way to Lexington. British patrols were out in force that night, according to writer O'Donnell. The British captured Revere and placed a pistol to his head and held him briefly, ordering him to tell what the colonial battle plans were.

''With deep regret it must be revealed that the great patriot spilled everything,'' claims writer O'Donnell. ''He gave such a detailed account of his glorious gallop that if Longfellow had only been there to take notes he might have written a more accurate poem.

Because they were busy trying to halt the revolution in its infancy, the British turned Paul loose after the questioning, not wanting to be bothered with prisoners. Revere did make it to Lexington to advise his two revolutionary friends, Samuel Adams and John Hancock to leave town.

The route Paul took to Lexington was not the same as he described. O'Donnell said that another rider, William Dawes, took the route that Revere reportedly rode, but nobody wrote a poem about Dawes, who, historically, seems to deserve at least equal credit for warning folk of the approaching British.

Regarding the matter of Paul's horse, which remains anonymous in history practically right up to now:

The little brown mare never was returned to her owner. A British officer kept the horse after arresting Revere, and nothing was ever seen of her again.

By the *Smithsonian* account, some historians claim the horse's name was Dobbin. Others say Scheherazade. A distinguished historian insisted the animal was named Sparky because Longfellow referred to ''the spark struck out by that steed in his flight.''

But the official genealogy of Deacon Larkin's family said the horse's name was ''Brown Beauty.'' So we hail thee, Brown Beauty, (and hope history corrects the anonymity).

PICK A WORD, ANY WORD

A new word game is giving Americans relief from the depressions of every day life.

Since words are our business, we'll share some with you.

''Deafchat'' was a creation of Editor Henry Gemmill of the *National Observer.* ''Deafchat'' is a conversation with nobody listening.

''Parentchutist'' is a Gemmill word for ''a person who bails out; after stacking the kids at day-care centers, they are left at night and on weekends with sitters.''

Predification . . . a forecast based on wishful thinking.''

Some other words Gemmill ''creactiveated'' include:

''TeleVapors''—The pract stupor induced by staring at the boob tube.

''Fatfolly''—The practice of sticking to a pretty strict diet except at the current meal.

''TerrorVision''—A typical evening TV program.

Gemmill caught the idea from Bernice Lewis, who is on leave as a teacher for the Baltimore schools. She calls it ''wordiary—the world of words.''

Other Lewisisms include:

''Peoply—About people; involving people; integrating people on a social basis. (Once we heard of a goose that got in a crowd and got ''peopled.'')

''Jesussonian''—One who follows the teaching of Jesus Christ.

''Malecular''—Great qualities of maleness, strength of character, responsibility, and endurance.

''Infernalize''—Seething internally; to nurture a loathing; to introvert with hostility and apathy.

Reading these two wordsmiths moved us to work up a few fitting our surroundings:

''Taxpuncture''—So-called painless revenue-raising.

''Oilmanac''—A New England consumer-ecologist.

''Triperiter''—What reporters use.

''Poortographer''—Makes bad pictures.

''Histrorney''—A no-good judge.

''Calumnist''—an irate columnist.

''Squealerdealer''—His trade fell flat.

''Cantselher''—A rejected suitor.

''Lepresentative''—An unpopular legislator.

''Sineater''—A moralist lawmaker.

''Sheporter''—A writerperson.

''Heporter''—A male chauvinist writer.

''BandagingEditor''—The fellow who tries to keep a newspaper staff working.